30 Days of Light

A 30-day creative practice designed for beginner to intermediate DSLR photographers. Explore the art of light through daily hands-on lessons, technical guidance, and mindful observation.

Learn to see light differently—and transform the way you make photographs.

30 Days of Light:
A Guided Photographic Journey to Seeing, Shaping, and Creating with Light

Carol Fox Henrichs

30 Days of Light A Guided Photographic Journey to Seeing, Shaping, and Creating with Light
© 2025 Carol Fox Henrichs
All rights reserved.

Published by Henrichs Media Group LLC
East-Central Texas, USA
www.cfh.art

Edited, written, and photographed by Carol Fox Henrichs
Design and layout by Carol Fox Henrichs

This book is a work of creative instruction. Every effort has been made to ensure accuracy and clarity. The author assumes no responsibility for errors, omissions, or outcomes related to the use of the material in this publication.

First Edition, 2025

For educational and personal use only. This publication is not intended to substitute for hands-on instruction or professional photography training.

Website: https://cfh.art

For inquiries, workshops, or permissions:
carol@cfh.art

About the Author

Carol Fox Henrichs is an award-winning fine art photographer, educator, and lifelong student of the natural world. Her creative work combines photographic craftsmanship with digital artistry, producing images that invite reflection and emotional connection. A native of Galveston Island and now based in east-central Texas, Carol's photography is deeply rooted in her love of nature, light, and visual storytelling.

Before dedicating herself full-time to photography, Carol spent over two decades teaching and leading instructional technology and digital learning initiatives in higher education. Today, she brings that same passion for learning and clarity to her photography workshops, which help students move beyond snapshots and into intentional image-making.

Her work has been exhibited widely and has inspired students across the country through classes, art shows, and speaking engagements.

To view more of her work, attend a workshop, or explore fine art prints, visit:
🌐 Website: https://cfh.art
▪️ Email: carol@cfh.art
📷 Instagram: @carolfoxhenrichsart
📘 Facebook: @carolfoxhenrichsart

Foreword

Photography has the power to reveal what we often overlook. And in my years behind the camera—and in the classroom—I've learned that the secret to stronger, more intentional photographs isn't always better gear or more editing. It's learning to see the light.

30 Days of Light was born from a desire to guide others toward that discovery. Whether you're just picking up your first DSLR/mirrorless camera or you've been shooting for years and want to reconnect with the fundamentals, this book offers a path through observation, exploration, and creativity.

These lessons reflect not only my personal photographic journey but also the hundreds of conversations I've had with students learning to trust their eye and express their voice. Each day builds on the last, not just in technical knowledge, but in confidence and curiosity.

While I used AI tools to help shape and organize this content, and help with grammar/spelling, the vision, direction, and expertise shared here are entirely my own. I designed these lessons to reflect how I teach, how I see, and how I encourage others to grow—not by chasing perfection, but by showing up with intention.

Thank you for letting me be part of your journey. Let's go find the light.

—Carol Fox Henrichs

Welcome to 30 Days of Light

Dear Photo Artist,

Whether you've just picked up your first camera or you've been shooting for a while and want to strengthen your foundation, I'm thrilled you're here. *30 Days of Light* is a guided journey designed to help you understand one of the most powerful elements in photography: light. Not just how to use it—but how to truly see it.

Over the course of my career as an award-winning photographer, I've spent years exploring the ways light can transform a subject, define a mood, and tell a story. But it wasn't just through taking photos that I developed this perspective—it was also through teaching photography to others. After more than two decades of guiding students at all levels, I've seen firsthand what unlocks confidence behind the camera: a mix of technical understanding, creative play, and mindful observation.

That's exactly what this book offers.

Each of the 30 daily lessons is hands-on and practical. You won't just read about photography—you'll do it. Every day gives you a clear objective, step-by-step instructions, and plenty of space to experiment. You don't need fancy gear or perfect weather. You just need curiosity, a camera, and a little time each day to explore.
This book is for:

- •Beginners who want to move past "lucky shots" and into intentional photography
- •Intermediate photographers ready to refine their skills and deepen their creative voice
- •Anyone seeking a structured but flexible challenge to improve their photography through daily practice

You can follow the program in 30 straight days, pace it weekly, or pick it up when inspiration strikes. There's no wrong way to work through it—only forward momentum.

As you move through these lessons, you'll not only gain technical skill—you'll start seeing light differently in your everyday world. And once you do, your photography will change forever.

I'm honored to be your guide on this path. Let's begin.

Warmly,
Carol

Table of Contents

Getting Started: What You'll Need (and What You Won't)

Before you dive into the first lesson, here's a quick guide to help you feel prepared. You don't need a studio, a shelf full of gear, or even perfect weather—you just need a camera and a willingness to observe. I'll walk you through what helps, what's optional, and what to keep in mind as you begin.

Your Camera

This book is designed for photographers using a DSLR, mirrorless, or any camera that allows manual control over aperture, shutter speed, and ISO. If you're using a more advanced compact camera with manual or semi-manual settings, you can still follow along.

You do not need the latest model or expensive gear. I've created some of my favorite images with mid-range cameras and a single lens. What matters most is how you use the tool—not how flashy it is.

"It's not the wand-- It's the wizard"

Recommended Settings and Modes

Throughout this book, we'll explore creative and technical control. I often suggest shooting in:

- Aperture Priority (A or Av mode) – great for controlling depth of field

- Manual Mode (M) – ideal once you get comfortable with balancing exposure

- Shutter Priority (S or Tv) – helpful for motion-related exercises

If you're brand new to these settings, don't worry—I'll ease you in, one concept at a time.

Lenses

Start with whatever lens you have. That said, here's what I personally find useful:

- A standard zoom (like 18–55mm or 24–70mm) covers a lot of ground
- A prime lens (like 50mm f/1.8) is excellent for low light and beautiful background blur
- A macro lens is fun for detail work, but not required

This book focuses more on how to see and use light than on specialty gear.

Other Helpful Tools (Optional, but Handy)

- Tripod – Especially useful for long exposure or low light exercises
- Reflector – A white poster board or piece of foam core works just fine
- Remote shutter release or self-timer – Helps eliminate camera shake
- Notebook or journal – To track your ideas, reflections, or lighting observations
- RAW capture mode – If your camera allows it, shooting in RAW gives you more flexibility when editing

Getting to Know Your Camera

Before starting, I recommend reviewing your camera's manual (or a few online tutorials) to make sure you know how to:

- Change aperture, shutter speed, and ISO

- Switch between Auto, Aperture Priority, Shutter Priority, and Manual

- Change exposure compensation in aperture priority mode.

- Move focus point

- Adjust white balance

- Read your histogram

- Enable the rule of thirds grid (if available)

If that feels overwhelming, it's okay. You'll get familiar with it over time —and I'll walk you through many of these in the lessons ahead.

My Personal Advice Before You Begin

In my years teaching photography, I've noticed that new photographers often worry about doing things the right way. Let me reassure you: the most important thing is that you show up with curiosity.

You'll take some bad photos. I do, too. You'll also create some that surprise you. Let those be your teachers.

This is not a race or a test. It's a 30-day opportunity to observe the world differently—and to learn how light can help you tell stories, shape mood, and make your images feel like you.

Are you ready? Grab your camera, head toward the light (or the shadow), and let's begin.

30 Days of Light – Cheat Sheets

Quick Reference Guides from Carol Fox Henrichs

These cheat sheets are here to help you troubleshoot in the field, understand your tools, and make creative decisions with clarity. Tape them inside your camera bag or keep them handy in your phone.

Most of all, trust your instincts and practice with purpose. The more you work with light, the more it will start to feel like second nature.

Exposure Triangle Cheat Sheet

One of the most powerful tools in your creative toolbox is understanding how aperture, shutter speed, and ISO work together. Think of them like three legs of a tripod—change one, and the others shift to maintain balance.

Aperture (f/stop)

- Controls how much light enters the lens – related to what is actually in focus

- Affects depth of field (what's in focus)

- Small f-number (f/2.8) = more light, blurry background

- Large f-number (f/16) = less light, more of the scene in focus

Shutter Speed

- Controls how long the sensor is exposed to light – thus it is related to time

- Affects motion blur or sharpness

- Fast (1/1000 sec) = freezes motion

•Slow (1/30 sec and under) = shows motion or light trails (use tripod)

ISO

•Controls the sensor's sensitivity to light

•Affects brightness and image noise

•Low ISO (100–400) = clean image, needs more light

•High ISO (1600–3200+) = brighter in dark scenes, more grain/noise

 Tip from me: If I'm unsure where to start, for a stationary subject, I set my aperture first (for creative look), adjust shutter speed next, then raise ISO as needed to get the best exposure.

Shutter Speeds for Stopping Motion:

Subject in Motion	Minimum Recommended Shutter Speed	Suggested Starting Point
People Walking	1/125 sec	1/250 sec
People Running	1/250 sec	1/500 sec
Race Cars / Motor Sports	1/500 sec	1/1000 sec
Birds in Flight	1/1000 sec	1/2000 sec
Hummingbird Wings	1/2000 sec	1/4000 sec

Notes:

•These shutter speeds are recommended starting points. Adjust according to your lighting conditions, lens focal length, distance from the subject, and specific creative needs.

•Always test and review your shots to adjust your shutter speed as needed. Higher shutter speeds will require more light from a larger aperture or increased ISO.

- •Use Continuous Autofocus (AF-C or AI Servo) to keep moving subjects sharply focused.

White Balance Cheat Sheet

Light isn't just bright or dim—it has color temperature. The right white balance setting helps you keep colors accurate (or creatively off, if you choose!).

Common Presets:

- •Auto – Let the camera decide (usually decent, but not perfect)

- •Daylight (5200K) – For outdoor sun

- •Shade (7000K) – Warms up cool shadows

- •Cloudy (6000K) – Slightly warmer than daylight

- •Tungsten (3200K) – For indoor lamps; cools yellow-orange tones

- •Fluorescent (4000K) – Neutralizes greenish indoor lights

💡 I often leave mine on "Auto" because I shoot in RAW I adjust it in post processing. However setting it while shooting reduces the amount of post processing required. Want creative control? Try setting it manually in Kelvin mode.

Quick Lighting Scenarios & What to Try

Lighting Condition	Tips
Harsh midday sun	Backlight the subject, find open shade or create shade for the subject
Golden hour	Shoot with the sun behind for glow, or side-light for depth & texture
Overcast	Soft, even light—perfect for portraits, wildflowers
Window light	Great for still life and indoor portraits; side-light for mood
Low light / indoors	Use a tripod, open your aperture, raise ISO, and watch for mood
Mixed light sources	Choose which light to prioritize and adjust white balance accordingly

💡 Even "bad" light can be beautiful when you stop fighting it and start shaping it.

Composition with Light: A Quick Guide

- •Lead the eye with light. Where it's brightest is where we look first!

- •Use shadow to hide distractions and add mystery.

- •Frame with light—bright subjects against darker surroundings make impact.

- •Create contrast to define shape and emotion.

- •Look for patterns of light or repetition of shadows.

💡 I often ask myself: "Where's the light strongest—and what story does it help tell?"

Troubleshooting Quick Fixes

Photo too dark?

    •Open the aperture (lower/smaller f-number)

    •Slow down the shutter speed (Note: a basice understanding of fractions is essential (1/250 is slower than 1/1000)

    •Raise ISO – don't be afraid to increase the ISO. Depending on your camers, most noise introduced can be reduced or eliminated with software in post processing.

Photo too bright?

    •Close the aperture (higher/larger f-number)

    •Speed up the shutter

    •Lower ISO

Colors look off?

    •Adjust white balance (try a different preset or manual Kelvin setting) Most important if shooting in modes that create JPG files.

Too much motion blur?

    •Use a faster shutter speed

    •Raise ISO if needed to keep exposure balanced

💡 If I forget a setting, I breathe, reset, and check the histogram—not just the screen.

Glossary of Photography Terms

This glossary is designed to help new photographers better understand the key concepts and language used throughout the 30 Days of Light lessons.

Aperture – The opening in a lens through which light passes. Measured in f-stops (like f/2.8, f/5.6, f/16). A lower number means a larger opening, letting in more light and creating a shallower depth of field.

Backlighting – A lighting situation where the main source of light comes from behind the subject, often creating rim light or silhouettes.

Bracketing – Taking multiple shots of the same scene at different exposure settings to ensure at least one well-exposed image or to combine them later.

Bounced Light – Light that has been redirected off a surface (like a wall or reflector) to soften or reposition the light source.

Color Temperature – The color appearance of light, measured in Kelvin (K). Lower values (e.g., 3200K) are warm (orange/yellow); higher values (e.g., 7000K) are cool (blue).

Composition – How visual elements are arranged in a photograph. Good composition guides the viewer's eye and strengthens the image's impact.

Depth of Field (DOF) – The range of sharpness in a photo from foreground to background. Controlled by aperture.

Dynamic Range – The range of tones from the darkest shadows to the brightest highlights that a camera can capture.

Exposure – The amount of light that reaches the camera sensor. Controlled by the combination of aperture, shutter speed, and ISO.

Exposure Triangle – A term for the three settings that affect exposure: aperture, shutter speed, and ISO. Adjusting one affects the others.

Golden Hour – The period shortly after sunrise or before sunset when the light is soft, warm, and directional—ideal for photography.

Hard Light – Light that creates sharp, well-defined shadows. Usually comes from a small or direct source like the sun at midday.

Histogram – A graph that shows the tonal distribution in your photo, from shadows (left) to highlights (right).

ISO – A measure of the camera sensor's sensitivity to light. A low ISO (e.g., 100) gives clean images in bright light. A high ISO (e.g., 3200) helps in low light but may add grain/noise. The amount of noise is dependent upon your camera's sensor—so not all cameras produce the same levels of noise.

Manual Mode (M) – A camera mode where the photographer sets all exposure settings (aperture, shutter speed, ISO) manually.

Metering – The way your camera measures light in a scene to suggest or set exposure. Common types include evaluative, center-weighted, and spot metering.

Open Shade – Areas of soft, even lighting found just outside direct sunlight—ideal for portraits and even exposure.

RAW -- A RAW file is an unprocessed image straight from your camera's sensor. Unlike JPEGs, which are compressed and edited automatically in-camera, RAW files preserve all the original data, giving you far more control when editing exposure, color, white balance, and detail later on. I like to think of a RAW file as a digital negative—full of potential, waiting to be developed. Shooting in RAW lets you work with the most flexibility and quality, especially when photographing in tricky light or planning to fine-tune your images later.

Reflected Light – Light that bounces off surfaces (walls, ground, whiteboards) and softly illuminates the subject.

Rule of Thirds – A compositional guide where the frame is divided into thirds horizontally and vertically. Think tic-tac-toe grid. Key subjects are often placed at intersections for balance and interest. This is more of a guideline than a real rule.

Shutter Speed – The amount of time the camera's shutter remains open. A fast shutter speed freezes motion; a slow one creates motion blur or can be used to create light trails.

Silhouette – A dark shape or outline of a subject with no visible detail, usually created by backlighting.

Soft Light – Light that wraps gently around a subject, creating soft transitions and little to no harsh shadow. Found in cloudy conditions or from large, diffused sources.

White Balance – A camera setting that adjusts for the color of the light source to ensure accurate colors in the image.

Feel free to bookmark, print, or reference this glossary as you move through the lessons. New terms may feel overwhelming at first—but with practice, they'll become part of how you see and speak photography.

Lessons 1-7: Observing the Light

"Before you can begin to shape the light, you must learn to see it."

Photography, at its core, is about capturing light. But before you adjust settings or press the shutter, the first—and perhaps most important—skill you must develop is simply observing the light in the scene. Once you can see the light, you'll never photograph the same way again.

In this first week, we'll slow down and tune in. You'll start noticing how light shifts throughout the day, how it bounces off surfaces, softens through curtains, glows on skin, or slices through blinds. You'll become familiar with light's many personalities: bold and harsh, soft and diffuse, golden and romantic, or cool and distant.

These first seven lessons are designed to awaken your awareness. We'll explore:

- •The direction of light and how it defines shape and form

- •The difference between hard and soft light—and when to use each

- •The beauty of golden hour and the challenge of high noon

- •How to find magic even in the shadows

As a photographer and educator, I've watched countless students shift from frustration to confidence when they begin to see light not as something technical—but as something alive and expressive. That shift starts here.

Don't worry about perfect exposures or advanced techniques this week. Focus instead on slowing down, watching the light, and noticing its effect on the world around you.

Let's begin.

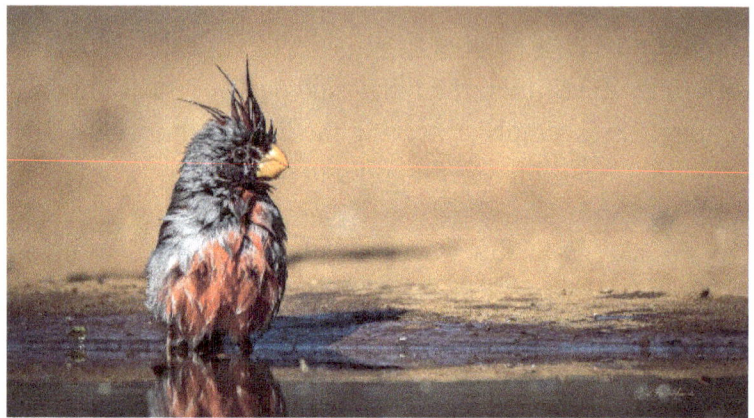

Day 1: Finding the Light

> "Before you raise the camera to your eye, learn to look at the light."

Why This Matters

Great photographs begin long before the shutter is pressed. They begin with seeing—truly seeing—the light. Light is the language of photography. It defines shape, texture, color, mood, and meaning. Whether you're photographing a person, a flower, or a crumbling building, the impact of your image hinges on the quality and direction of the light that illuminates it.

As a beginner, it's tempting to focus on gear or camera settings. But even the best equipment won't make an image compelling if the light is flat or uninteresting. Learning to observe and understand light is the first step to consistently creating powerful photographs. Once you train your eyes to notice light—its softness or harshness, where it's coming from, and how it changes throughout the day—you'll find that you start seeing photographic possibilities *everywhere*.

What You'll Learn Today

- How to observe natural light in everyday settings
- The difference between hard and soft light
- How to identify the direction of light and use it creatively
- Why quality and direction of light influence emotional tone and visual clarity

Step-by-Step Exercise: Find the Light

You will work with one subject and photograph it under different lighting conditions throughout a single day. This helps you develop awareness of how dramatically light influences your scene.

What You Need

- •A DSLR or mirrorless camera (shoot in Aperture Priority or Manual mode)
- •One simple subject: a mug, plant, figurine, or any small object
- •A window with indirect sunlight (ideally east- or west-facing)
- •A notebook or app for notes

Step 1: Choose Your Subject and Location

Select a small object with texture or shape. Place it near a window in a room where you can revisit it during the day. Avoid using artificial light —this is about learning from natural light only.

Step 2: Observe Morning Light

Visit your subject within 1–2 hours after sunrise. Spend at least 5 minutes simply looking before you photograph anything.

Ask yourself:

- •Is the light warm or cool in tone?
- •Are the shadows long or soft?
- •What direction is the light coming from?
- •What parts of your subject are most lit or most in shadow?

Take a few photos. Note the time of day and what you observe.

Step 3: Observe Midday Light

Return around midday, when the sun is high. Even though indoor light may appear bright, it's often cooler and harsher now.

Questions to ask:

- •Is the light stronger or more neutral now?
- •Are shadows deeper and harder?
- •How do details look compared to this morning?

Photograph your subject again. If you are shooting in Aperture Priority mode, try adjusting your exposure compensation if needed (start with +1/3 or +2/3 stop).

Step 4: Observe Late Afternoon or Golden Hour Light

Come back within the last 2 hours before sunset. This is often the most photogenic light of the day.

Observe:

- •Is the light warmer or more angled?
- •Are shadows longer and softer?
- •How does the subject's mood change compared to earlier?

Take a few final shots. Consider photographing from a different angle to play with direction.

Step 5: Review and Reflect

Now import your images and look at them side by side. Notice:

- •Which image feels more emotionally engaging?
- •Where does the eye go first in each image?
- •How does the quality and direction of light change the story your photo tells?

Write a short reflection on which time of day best suited your subject—and why.

Key Concepts to Remember

1. Quality of Light

• Soft Light is diffused, low contrast, and forgiving. It often comes from cloudy skies, window shade, or during golden hour. It wraps gently around subjects.

• Hard Light is direct and casts strong shadows. It adds drama, but can also exaggerate flaws or create distracting contrasts.

2. Direction of Light

• Front Light (light behind you): Even exposure, flat look, low shadows.

• Side Light (light from left or right): Adds depth, reveals texture, creates contrast.

• Back Light (light behind the subject): Can create silhouettes, halos, or glow.

• Top Light (overhead sun): Can cause harsh shadows under eyes or nose—often best avoided for portraits.

Why This Will Make Your Photos Better

Learning to observe light gives you control. Instead of reacting to a scene, you start making intentional choices. You can wait for better light, move your subject, or change your angle to use the light creatively. *This is what separates snapshot-takers from thoughtful image-makers.*

Most importantly, you'll begin to feel the light. You'll walk into a room and know where the best photo will be. You'll stand in a forest and instantly see which beam of sunlight turns an ordinary branch into poetry.

Bonus Tip: Train Your Eye Daily

Start narrating the light around you, even without a camera.

• "The sun is creating rim light on that tree."

- "This hallway is softly lit by bounce from the floor."
- "The light here is flat and needs contrast."

Make light your constant companion—and you'll never see the world the same way again.

Final Thought

Today wasn't about making the perfect photo—it was about beginning a habit of looking. Every great image starts with light, and the more you train your eye to notice it—how it falls, where it comes from, what it touches—the more natural and intuitive your photography will become.

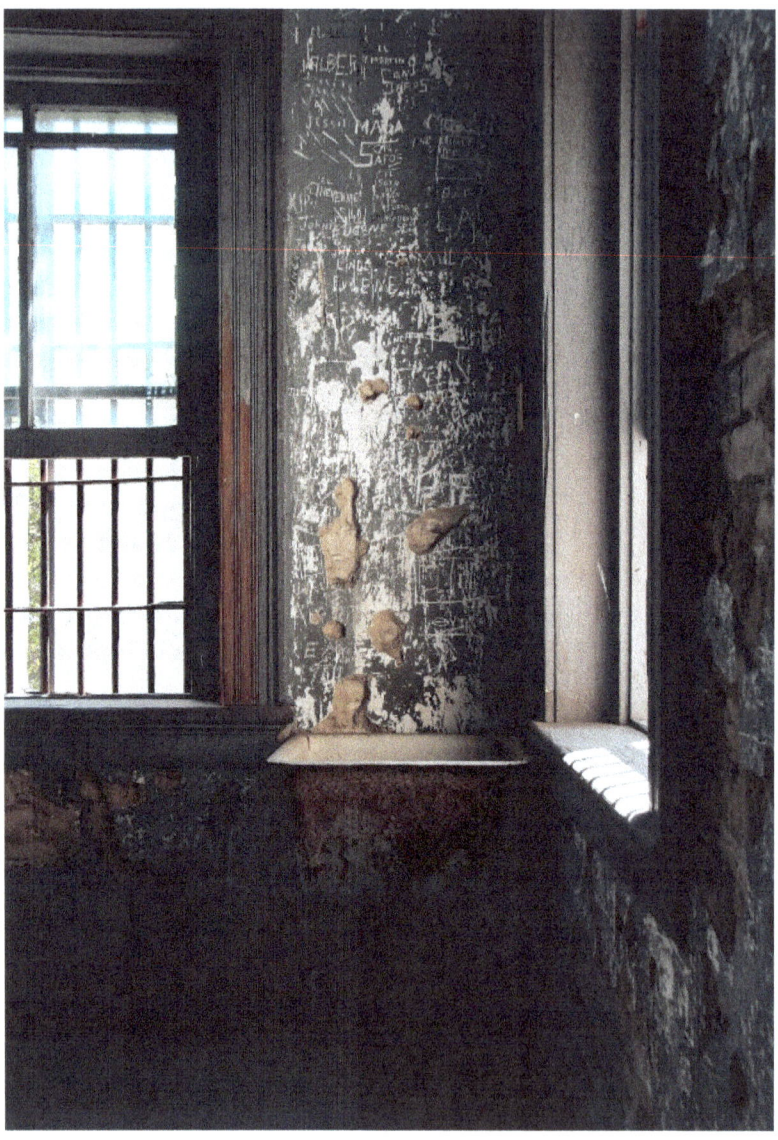

I made this image, inside a historic jail in Gonzales, TX. The light tells the story. The soft beams of mid-afternoon light, spill through the barred window, cutting through the darkness and falling gently across the etched graffiti left by former prisoners—words and marks carved into the wall as quiet declarations of existence. The surrounding shadows are deep and undisturbed, allowing the viewer's eye to be drawn immediately to where the light lands. This is a perfect example of observing natural light with intention, the core of Day 1. I didn't alter or add light—I simply watched, waited, and positioned myself to capture the way light revealed something easily overlooked. It's not just a photo of a place—it's a photo of what the light chose to show me.

Day 1 Reflective Journal Pages

Use these prompts to reflect after each lesson or at the end of each week. There's no right or wrong way to answer—let your thoughts flow honestly and creatively.

Day 1: Finding the Light

1. What did I observe about the light today?

2. What surprised or challenged me during this lesson?

3. Which image felt the strongest—and why?

4. What would I do differently if I repeated this exercise?

5. Notes, thoughts, or ideas sparked today:

[Space for writing or sketching]

Day 2: Hard vs. Soft Light

"The light is not just what we see—it's what we feel in a photograph."

Why This Matters

Understanding the quality of light—whether it's hard or soft—is essential for crafting compelling images. The quality of light determines the mood of your photo, how your subject is revealed, and how your viewer emotionally connects with the scene.

Soft light whispers. It wraps gently around your subject, reducing shadows and giving a delicate, dreamy quality to portraits, still life, or florals. Hard light, on the other hand, shouts. It's bold, contrasty, and full of drama. It works well for architecture, strong shapes, and when you want to emphasize grit or edge.

As a photographer, learning to recognize and harness both types of light gives you creative freedom. You're no longer at the mercy of lighting conditions—you know how to make the most of them.

What You'll Learn Today

- •How to recognize hard and soft light
- •When to use each type for creative impact
- •How to modify light to change its quality
- •How to photograph the same subject in both types of light for comparison

Step-by-Step Exercise: Hard vs. Soft Light

You'll photograph the same subject under both hard and soft lighting conditions and compare the results.

What You Need

- •Your DSLR or mirrorless camera
- •One textured object (e.g., a face, flower, rock, or fruit)
- •Access to direct sunlight and open shade
- •Optional: white reflector or large sheet of paper

Step 1: Set Up in Hard Light

Find a place outdoors or indoors where direct sunlight falls on your subject. This is your hard light environment.

✒Tip: Midday sun or direct window light creates the hardest light.

- •Place your subject in the full beam of light.
- •Observe the shadows. Are they sharp-edged? High in contrast?
- •Take a few photos, exposing for the highlights (use exposure compensation if needed).
- •Try changing your angle—how does the shape and intensity of shadow shift?

Note the time of day and light direction.

Step 2: Set Up in Soft Light

Now, move your subject into open shade (find a porch-like structure or make a porch over the subject) or shoot at a time when the sun is diffused by clouds.

📌 Tip: North-facing windows, shaded porches, or cloudy skies offer soft light.

- Look at the shadows again. Are they faint or almost nonexistent?
- Does the texture appear flatter or more even?
- Take a few photos, adjusting exposure as needed (you may need to increase ISO or widen aperture).

Note how the mood changes between these two lighting conditions.

Step 3: Modify the Light (Optional Advanced Step)

To experience how light quality can be modified, try these:

- Use a sheer curtain or white shower curtain to diffuse hard light and make it soft.
- Use a white board, paper, or reflector to bounce light and fill in shadows.
- Try placing a black card opposite the light source to deepen shadows for more contrast.

Take comparison shots and label which images were modified.

Step 4: Review and Compare

Upload or view your images side by side.

Ask yourself:

- Which photo has more dramatic contrast? Which feels gentler?
- How does light quality change the texture and mood of your subject?
- Where do your eyes go first in each image?

Bonus reflection: Which type of light better serves your subject—and why?

Key Concepts to Remember

Hard Light

- •Source: Direct sunlight, unfiltered flash, spotlight
- •Shadows: Dark and well-defined
- •Mood: Dramatic, harsh, edgy, graphic
- •Best For: Architecture, strong shapes, gritty portraits, high-contrast scenes

Soft Light

- •Source: Cloudy skies, shade, diffused window light
- •Shadows: Light or barely visible
- •Mood: Calm, dreamy, flattering
- •Best For: Portraits, flowers, still life, evenly lit scenes

Why This Will Make Your Photos Better

Photographers who understand light quality don't just take pictures—they shape their images before even pressing the shutter. They anticipate how their subject will look under different conditions, and they choose light with purpose.

You'll begin to notice:

- •Why some portraits look professional and others feel harsh
- •How the same flower can seem elegant or eerie based on light quality
- •That you don't need a studio—just smart observation and positioning

Once you master this, you're already thinking like a photographer.

Quick Daily Practice

For the next week, as you go about your day:

- Identify examples of hard and soft light in your environment

- Ask: What kind of shadows do I see?

- Mentally label the light: This is soft. This is hard.

Final Thought

Light is never "bad." It's only inappropriate for your subject or your intent. By understanding the difference between hard and soft light, you're already taking control of your images—and that's where great photography begins.

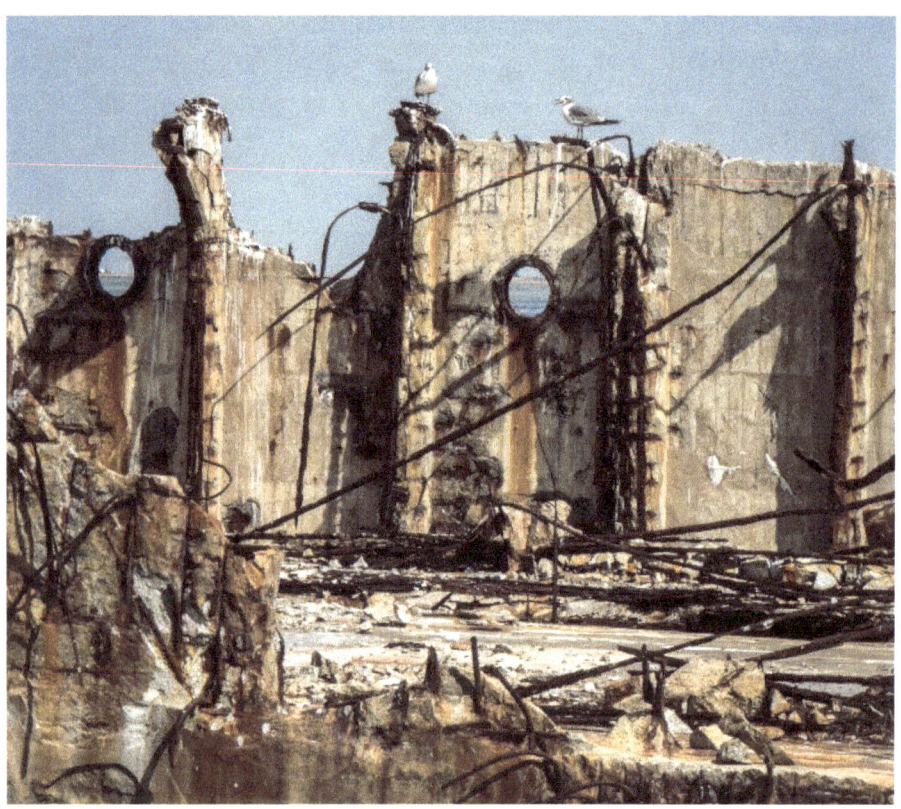

This is my photograph, taken off the coast of Galveston Island. It captures the weathered remains of a sunken concrete ship under the unfiltered glare of strong, mid-day sun. The hard light casts sharp, well-defined shadows that emphasize the jagged lines of exposed rebar and the rough, pitted texture of the aging concrete. Every crack, edge, and detail is brought into high relief—showing how hard light can be used intentionally to reveal structure, grit, and form. While softer light might have subdued the scene, this photo embraces the starkness and uses it to convey the harsh reality of decay and time. It's a visual study in how the quality of light can shape the emotional tone of an image—turning broken remains into something visually bold and striking.

Day 2 Reflective Journal Pages

Use these prompts to reflect after each lesson or at the end of each week. There's no right or wrong way to answer—let your thoughts flow honestly and creatively.

Day 2: Hard vs. Soft Light

1. What did I observe about the light today?

2. What surprised or challenged me during this lesson?

3. Which image felt the strongest—and why?

4. What would I do differently if I repeated this exercise?

5. Notes, thoughts, or ideas sparked today:

[Space for writing or sketching]

Day 3: Golden Hour Magic

> "Golden hour is nature's most flattering light—
> gentle, warm, and full of promise."

Why This Matters

Ask any seasoned photographer when to shoot and you'll likely hear: "Golden hour." This refers to the short window of time just after sunrise and just before sunset when the sun is low on the horizon. The light during golden hour is soft, warm, and directional—perfect for adding atmosphere and emotional resonance to your images.

Unlike the harsh midday sun that flattens detail and creates deep shadows, golden hour light wraps your subject in a glow. It enhances skin tones, gives landscapes a magical warmth, and adds depth through long shadows and gentle highlights. Knowing how—and when—to harness this light is one of the most useful tools in a photographer's creative kit.

What You'll Learn Today

- •What golden hour light is and when it occurs
- •How to plan your shoot to capture it
- •How golden hour affects color, contrast, and emotion
- •Three different lighting approaches during golden hour: front light, side light, and back light

Step-by-Step Exercise: Golden Hour Three Ways

You'll shoot the same subject using three lighting angles during golden hour to explore how directional light transforms a scene.

What You Need

- Your DSLR or mirrorless camera

- A subject (a person, pet, landscape feature, or object—ideally something outdoors)

- A location with a clear view of the low horizon

- A timing app or weather app to find sunrise/sunset times

- Optional: tripod, reflector

Step 1: Plan Your Shoot

Use an app like PhotoPills, Sun Surveyor, or even a weather app to look up the sunrise or sunset time in your area.

- Morning golden hour: Begins shortly after sunrise

- Evening golden hour: Begins about one hour before sunset

Arrive early—light changes quickly. Pick a location with a subject that won't move (e.g., a tree, a person you can direct, a flowerbed, or interesting architecture).

Step 2: Shoot with Front Light

- Position yourself with the sun behind you, shining directly on your subject.

- This results in even, warm light with low shadows.

- Expose for the subject's highlights. Use the histogram to ensure highlights are not bunching along the right side.

- Ideal for flattering portraits or vibrant colors in landscapes.

Take 2–3 shots with minor variations in angle and distance to the subject.

Step 3: Shoot with Side Light

•Rotate around your subject until the sun is hitting it from the left or right side.

•Notice how shadows fall, enhancing shape and texture.

•This lighting is more dramatic and can add depth and contrast.

•Be mindful of your exposure—meter for midtones. To achieve balanced exposure in your images, it helps to meter for the midtones—the areas of your scene that aren't the brightest highlights or the deepest shadows, but fall somewhere in between. These midtones often carry the most detail and set the overall mood of the photograph.

Here's how to do it:

1.Switch to Spot or Center-Weighted Metering Mode: These modes give you more control by prioritizing a specific part of the frame rather than averaging the entire scene.

2.Identify a Midtone Area: Look for something in the scene that is a neutral or middle value—like a green lawn, weathered wood, a gray rock, or even light skin tone in soft light. Avoid very bright or very dark areas.

3.Point Your Camera at the Midtone: Aim your focus/metering point at that midtone area. If your camera lets you lock exposure (AE-L), press that button to hold the exposure setting. If not, take a mental note of the settings your camera chooses.

4.Recompose and Shoot: With exposure set based on the midtones, reframe your composition if needed and take the photo. Metering for the midtones helps prevent blown-out highlights and overly dark shadows, giving you a more balanced file to work with in post-processing. It's a foundational skill that supports creative decisions—whether you want to preserve detail or deliberately push exposure for a high-key or low-key look.

Take several shots and adjust position slightly to see how it changes the mood.

Step 4: Shoot with Back Light

- •Now place your subject between you and the sun.
- •This creates a glow or halo effect, especially if your subject has translucent parts (hair, petals, leaves).
- •You may need to use exposure compensation (+1 or +2 stops) to avoid your subject turning into a silhouette—unless that's your intention.
- •Optional: Use a reflector or white card to bounce light back onto the subject's face or front.

Take a few exposures with and without compensation. Try creative focus for dreamy effects. Let go of the need for tack-sharp precision and explore how softness can tell a different kind of story. Selective focus, intentional blur, and shallow depth of field can all introduce a gentle, ethereal mood to your images. Shift your focus just slightly—perhaps to a single petal, a blade of grass, or even beyond your subject—and notice how the background melts into a wash of color and light. This technique isn't about technical perfection; it's about evoking emotion, mystery, and wonder. Think of it as painting with your lens rather than documenting with it.

Step 5: Review and Compare

Load your images into your editing software or review on your camera.

Ask yourself:

- •Which direction of light feels most emotionally engaging?
- •Where are shadows helping or hurting?
- •How do colors differ between the three approaches?
- •Which version best tells a story?

Jot down your preferences and thoughts.

Key Concepts to Remember

Golden Hour Light

- Tone: Warm, reddish-golden

- Quality: Soft, low contrast

- Direction: Sun is low, casting long shadows and subtle highlights

- Mood: Romantic, peaceful, nostalgic, magical

Light Directions Recap

- Front Light: Colors pop; detail is clear (as long as the light is not too harsh); minimal texture

- Side Light: Depth and drama; enhanced texture

- Back Light: Glow, silhouettes, mystery, or mood

Why This Will Make Your Photos Better

Learning to work with golden hour light trains you to see light creatively. You'll learn to anticipate its quality, chase it, and use it intentionally. Your images will instantly feel more polished, painterly, and professional—even without complex equipment or editing.

Even more importantly, golden hour helps you slow down. You become more attuned to the light's changing temperature, direction, and intensity. That sense of awareness is what leads to consistently stronger photographs, no matter the subject.

Quick Daily Practice

- Observe golden hour from a porch or a window: Where is the light warmest or the shadows the longest? Try photographing the same scene at golden hour and again at midday to compare the difference in tone and mood.

Final Thought

Golden hour is a gift from the universe to photographers. But it's fleeting. The more you practice working with it, the more instinctive your timing, camera settings, and compositions will become.

So tomorrow morning—or this evening—go chase the light.

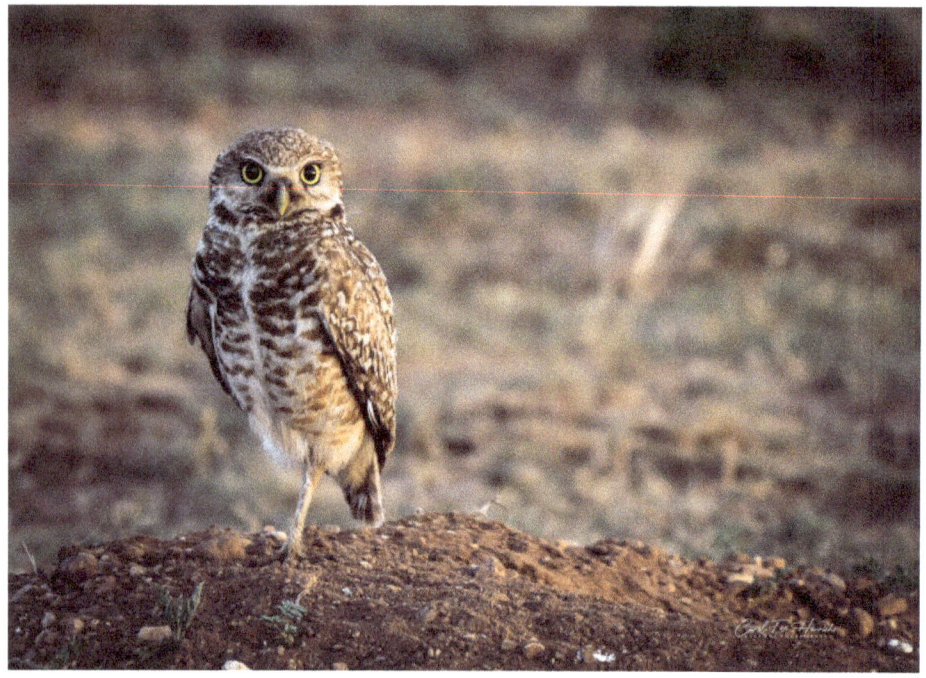

I captured this image of a Burrowing Owl (balancing on one leg), during the golden hour, while it was bathed in the soft, warm light of early morning. The sun, still low on the horizon, wraps the owl in a gentle glow that enhances the rich browns and subtle patterns of its feathers. This photo perfectly embodies the principles explored in Day 3—how golden hour light softens details, adds warmth, and elevates even simple scenes with a sense of quiet magic. The light doesn't just illuminate the owl—it enhances its presence, creating an inviting and intimate atmosphere. It's a moment that feels both wild and peaceful, captured in the kindest light of the day.

Day 3 Reflective Journal Pages

Use these prompts to reflect after each lesson or at the end of each week. There's no right or wrong way to answer—let your thoughts flow honestly and creatively.

Day 3: Golden Hour Magic

1. What did I observe about the light today?

2. What surprised or challenged me during this lesson?

3. Which image felt the strongest—and why?

4. What would I do differently if I repeated this exercise?

5. Notes, thoughts, or ideas sparked today:

[Space for writing or sketching]

Day 4: Shade and Open Shadow

"Shade doesn't mean dull. In fact, it can reveal beauty that bright light hides."

Why This Matters

When you're starting out, it's easy to think that more light equals better photos. But some of the most beautiful, nuanced images are made in less light—specifically, in shade and open shadow.

Shade provides soft, even illumination. It removes the harsh contrasts of direct sunlight and lets the subtle colors, textures, and details of your subject shine. Skin tones become more flattering, colors appear truer, and shadows are gentle rather than distracting. Open shadow—the area just outside the edge of direct light—gives you the benefits of shade while still catching some ambient brightness.

Learning how to see and use shade expands your creative toolbox. You'll be able to make strong images even in the middle of a bright, contrast-heavy day—just by moving a few feet into the shadows.

What You'll Learn Today

- How to identify good quality shade and open shadow
- How to adjust exposure for shaded scenes
- When and why to choose shade for portraits, close-ups, and color-rich subjects
- How to balance ambient light and directional light in shaded environments

Step-by-Step Exercise: Seeing in the Shade

Today, you'll photograph a subject in both full sun and in shade, comparing how light quality affects your image—and your exposure.

What You Need
- •DSLR or mirrorless camera
- •One subject (a person, flower, textured object, or even your hand)
- •A location with both open sunlight and shaded areas (e.g., side of a building, tree canopy, porch)
- •Optional: White card or reflector

Step 1: Photograph in Direct Sunlight (for Comparison)

Place your subject in direct sunlight and take a few photos.

- •Observe the brightness, contrast, and sharpness of shadows.
- •Pay attention to how the highlights might look blown out or overly bright.

This step gives you a baseline for comparison—don't skip it.

Step 2: Move into the Shade

Now, place your subject just outside the sunlit area—in open shade. This might be under a tree, beside a building, or beneath an awning.

📌 Tip: Open shade is often brighter and more colorful than deep shade. Look for a shaded area that still receives reflected light from nearby surfaces (e.g., light pavement, walls, or sky).

- •Notice how the light softens, shadows become diffused, and details are easier to see.
- •Adjust your exposure compensation to +1/3 or +2/3 if the image looks too dark—your camera is metering the darker scene and may underexpose it. Refer to your camera documentation for exposure compensation in aperture priority mode.

•Use a wide aperture (like f/2.8 to f/5.6) to let in more light.

Take several shots from different angles. Focus on the evenness of tone and the subtlety of color.

Step 3: Modify or Enhance Shade

Try adding or manipulating the light in the shaded scene:

•Use a reflector or white card to bounce ambient light back onto the subject.

•Position your subject so that light is coming in from one direction (e.g., from a nearby bright wall or patch of sky) to maintain shape and avoid flatness.

•Try moving deeper into the shade to compare open vs. deep shadow.

Take a few more photos with and without the reflector/modifier.

Step 4: Review and Compare

Look at your direct sun vs. shade vs. modified shade photos.

Ask:

•Which image shows more detail in both shadows and highlights?
•How does the subject's color change in each light?
•Which version feels more natural or visually pleasing?

Make a few notes about which shaded environments gave you the best light—and why.

Key Concepts to Remember

Shade (and Open Shadow)

- •Light Quality: Soft, low contrast, evenly distributed
- •Color: Truer tones without overexposure
- •Mood: Calm, quiet, gentle
- •Best For: Portraits, flowers, food, close-ups, mid-day shooting

Tips for Working in Shade

- •Look for reflected light sources to add brightness and dimension.
- •Use exposure compensation to avoid underexposed images.
- •Add shape by working near a directional source (window, patch of sky, reflective surface).

Why This Will Make Your Photos Better

Shooting in shade is one of the easiest ways to instantly improve image quality—especially for portraits and detailed subjects. It removes harsh shadows, helps avoid blown highlights, and keeps your viewer focused on what matters.

Once you develop an eye for open shadow, you'll stop fighting the sun. Instead of avoiding photography during bright midday hours, you'll start using shade as a reliable, natural softbox.

Quick Daily Practice

As you go about your day, look for areas of open shade:

- •Under a tree canopy

- Along the side of a building

- Beneath a porch roof or pavilion

Observe:

- How colors appear richer?

- How soft the shadows become?

- How the subject remains well-lit but without harshness?

Final Thought

Shade isn't boring—it's subtle. It asks you to look a little closer, to notice the quiet beauty of soft light, and to trust that calm and control can be just as powerful as drama. Use it to your advantage, and your photography will feel more intentional and refined.

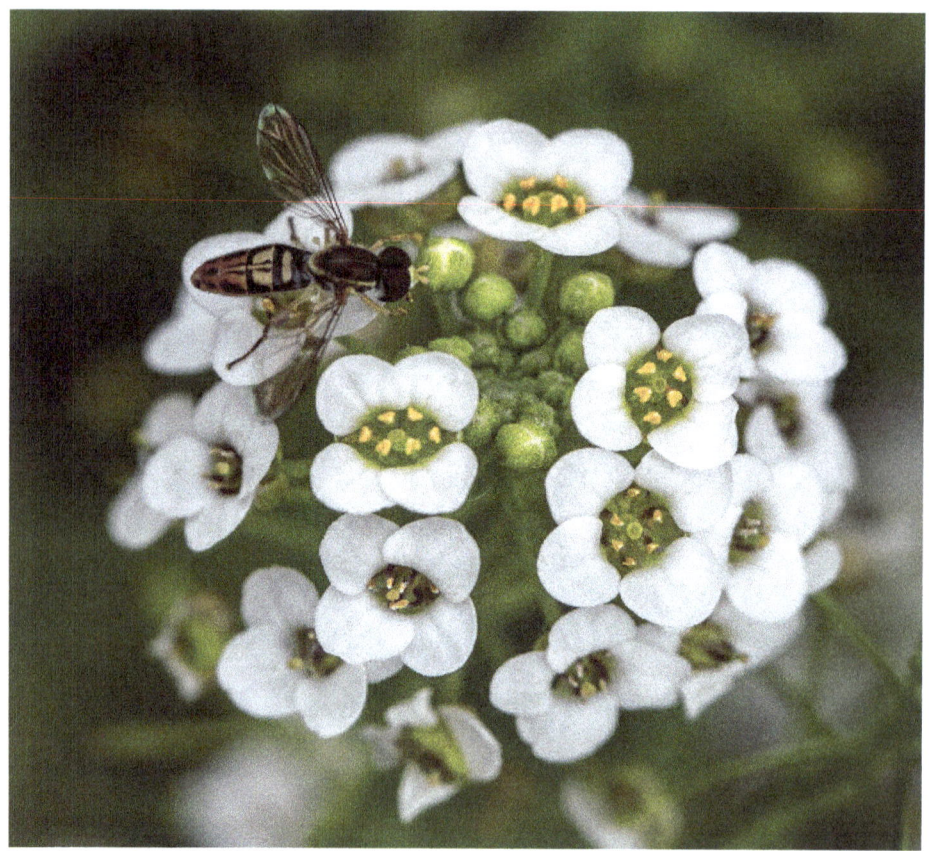

This Sweet Alyssum was growing in my north-facing flowerbed. The eaves of the house created a nice shady spot for this photo. The result is a perfect example of open shade—an environment where light is soft, even, and indirect. In this kind of light, shadows are subtle, highlights aren't blown out, and fine details—like the delicate petals and soft textures of the flowers—can be captured without harsh contrast. Day 4 encourages us to recognize that shade isn't a lack of light, but a tool for control and subtlety. Here, the shaded light allowed me to preserve the natural softness of the scene, creating an image that feels calm and true to life. It's a quiet reminder that sometimes the best light is the kind you almost don't notice.

Day 4 Reflective Journal Pages

Use these prompts to reflect after each lesson or at the end of each week. There's no right or wrong way to answer—let your thoughts flow honestly and creatively.

Day 4: Shade and Open Shadow

1. What did I observe about the light today?

2. What surprised or challenged me during this lesson?

3. Which image felt the strongest—and why?

4. What would I do differently if I repeated this exercise?

5. Notes, thoughts, or ideas sparked today:

[Space for writing or sketching]

Day 5: Backlighting Basics

"Sometimes the most beautiful light is the one you can't see—until it surrounds your subject from behind."

Why This Matters

Backlighting is when the main source of light comes from behind your subject, facing into your camera. While it might seem counterintuitive to photograph into the light, backlighting can produce some of the most magical effects in photography: glowing edges, luminous hair, translucent petals, and rich atmospheric mood.

Beginners often shy away from backlighting because it can be technically tricky—exposure is harder to manage, and autofocus may struggle. But once you learn how to work with it, backlighting becomes one of your most expressive tools. It adds drama, softness, mystery, or glow, depending on how you use it.

What You'll Learn Today

- How to recognize strong backlight
- How to expose for your subject, not the background
- How to use backlight for rim lighting, glow, and mood
- How to avoid common mistakes with lens flare and underexposure

Step-by-Step Exercise: Photographing with Backlight

You'll photograph a subject using backlight, experiment with exposure compensation, and learn to work with glow and rim light.

What You Need

- •DSLR or mirrorless camera

- •A subject (person, flower, leaf, glass, or textured object)

- •A location with low or angled sunlight (morning or late afternoon is best)

- •Optional: Reflector, white paper, lens hood

Step 1: Identify Your Light Source

Look for a light source behind your subject:

- •The sun low in the sky
- •A bright window behind a still life setup
- •A lamp or candle (for indoor practice)

📌 Golden hour is ideal for soft backlight—-it is also possible for you to work with midday light filtered through trees or curtains.

Position yourself facing the light, with your subject between you and the light source.

Step 2: Frame and Observe

Take a moment to look at your subject:

- •Is there a halo of light around the edges?
- •Are translucent areas glowing (like flower petals or hair)?
- •Does the background appear brighter than the subject?

Now take a test photo. You may notice:

- •Your subject is too dark (underexposed)
- •The background is properly exposed but your subject becomes a silhouette

That's normal! Time to fix it.

Step 3: Adjust Exposure

To avoid silhouettes (unless you want one), you need to tell your camera to expose for the subject, not the background.

Option 1: Use Exposure Compensation

- •Set your camera to Aperture Priority or Program mode

- •Increase your exposure compensation to +1 or +2 stops

- •This brightens your subject while allowing the background to blow out slightly

Option 2: Use Spot Metering

- •Switch your metering mode to Spot

- •Aim your camera's focus point at the subject's face or most important feature

- •Take a photo and check the result

Take several shots at different compensation levels and metering options. Watch for detail in your subject without losing the overall glow.

Step 4: Control Flare (or Embrace It)

Backlight often produces lens flare—those hazy circles or foggy washes across your image. You can either minimize it or use it artistically.

To minimize flare:

- •Use a lens hood or your hand to shade the lens

- •Slightly reposition your camera angle to keep the sun just out of frame

To use flare artistically:

- •Shoot directly into the sun

- •Lower contrast and increase warmth in post-processing

- •Allow soft haze to create mood

Take a few images both ways—one clean and contrasty, one dreamy and full of flare.

Step 5: Add Fill Light (Optional)

To add detail to your subject's face or front:

•Use a reflector or a white board to bounce light back

•Or simply move your subject closer to a reflective surface (white wall, pavement)

Try one photo with and one without the added fill.

Review and Compare

Look at your final set of images and ask:

•Which exposure gave you the best balance between subject and background?

•Did the glow or flare add to the image—or distract?

•How did the emotion or atmosphere change with different approaches?

Write a short note about what you liked or struggled with—and what you'd like to try again.

Key Concepts to Remember

Backlighting Creates:

•Rim Light: A glowing edge around your subject's silhouette

•Glow: Soft light that seems to radiate through translucent materials

•Atmosphere: Dreamy or ethereal mood, especially during golden hour

•Silhouette: A graphic shape with no detail, if exposed for the background

Challenges:

•Subject often too dark → use exposure compensation

•Autofocus may hunt → switch to manual focus if needed

•Flare can reduce contrast → block light or reposition

Why This Will Make Your Photos Better

Backlighting adds emotion and visual poetry to your photography. It's how you make a simple portrait feel magical, how you turn a leaf into a glowing jewel, or how you give a quiet scene an otherworldly quality. By learning to expose correctly, manage flare, and use bounce light, you take control of a traditionally tricky situation—and use it to elevate your work beyond the ordinary.

Quick Daily Practice

•At sunrise or sunset, walk outside and notice which objects glow from behind.

•Practice seeing rim light on trees, fences, flowers, or people's hair.

•Photograph a leaf or flower with the sun behind it—just to practice glow and translucency.

Final Thought

Backlighting isn't just a technical challenge—it's a storytelling tool. It helps you convey tenderness, drama, mystery, or magic with just a change of angle. Learn to trust the light behind your subject, and your images will begin to feel illuminated from within.

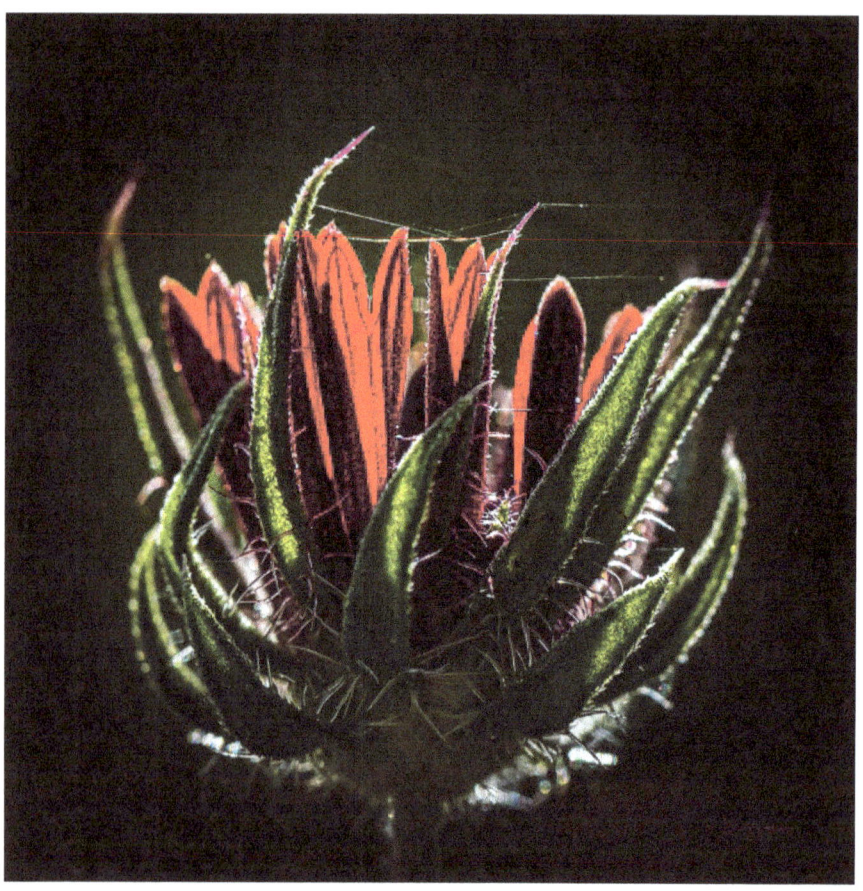

My photograph of a red blanket flower is a striking example of how backlighting can reveal the hidden beauty within a subject. With the light source behind the flower, the translucent petals glow with a rich, saturated red, and the fine veins become visible, like delicate lines in stained glass. The soft light also highlights the tiny hairs on the sepals, giving the image a subtle, luminous edge. As we explored in Day 5, backlighting is about more than just a dramatic silhouette—it's a technique that can illuminate texture, form, and structure in ways front or side lighting cannot. In this image, the backlight brings the flower to life from within, capturing both its fragility and brilliance in a single frame.

Day 5 Reflective Journal Pages

Use these prompts to reflect after each lesson or at the end of each week. There's no right or wrong way to answer—let your thoughts flow honestly and creatively.

Day 5: Backlighting Basics

1. What did I observe about the light today?

2. What surprised or challenged me during this lesson?

3. Which image felt the strongest—and why?

4. What would I do differently if I repeated this exercise?

5. Notes, thoughts, or ideas sparked today:

[Space for writing or sketching]

Day 6: High Noon Contrast

"When the sun is at its strongest, so is the contrast—
bold, unforgiving, and full of creative potential."

Why This Matters

Most photographers are told to avoid shooting at midday—and for good reason. When the sun is high overhead, shadows fall straight down, highlights become harsh, and your camera struggles to hold detail in both light and dark areas. This is called high contrast lighting, and it's often seen as difficult or unflattering.

But learning to work with high noon light teaches you control, adaptability, and boldness. Instead of running from the sun, you'll learn how to lean into its extremes and use it to create powerful, graphic images. Whether you're photographing architecture, strong textures, black & white compositions, or dramatic portraits, midday contrast can become one of your most striking tools—once you know how to handle it.

What You'll Learn Today

- •What makes high noon light difficult—and how to work with it
- •How to expose for highlights or shadows depending on your subject
- •How to embrace contrast for black & white or high-drama effects
- •Creative ways to soften or redirect hard midday light

Step-by-Step Exercise: Photographing in High Contrast Light

You'll photograph a scene in full midday sun, expose for different parts of the image, and experiment with how contrast changes composition and emotion.

What You Need

- Your DSLR or mirrorless camera
- A subject with distinct shape or texture (e.g., building, sculpture, rough surface, bold shadows)
- Outdoor location at midday (between 11 a.m. and 2 p.m.)
- Optional: white card or small diffuser
- Black & white setting (or shoot in RAW and convert later)

Step 1: Find a High-Contrast Subject

Look for scenes with:

- Bright light and deep shadow
- Strong lines or architectural details
- Interesting cast shadows from trees, fences, people, or buildings

📌 Tip: I find that sidewalks, stairwells, and city streets often offer great patterns of light and dark at midday.

Step 2: Expose for the Highlights

Start by setting your camera to Aperture Priority or Manual mode.

- Point your camera at the brightest area of the scene.

- Adjust your settings or use exposure compensation (-1 to -2 stops) to preserve highlight detail.

- Take a photo and check the histogram. You want to avoid clipping (losing) detail in the highlights.

This version will likely make the shadows very dark or completely black —a dramatic effect, especially for graphic compositions.

Step 3: Expose for the Shadows

Now do the opposite:

- Adjust exposure so the shadowed areas reveal detail.

- Use exposure compensation (+1 to +2 stops) if needed.

- Be aware that this may blow out the highlights (they'll turn pure white)—and that's okay for some styles.

This version shows more midtone detail but sacrifices brightness. It may feel softer or more mysterious.

Step 4: Convert to Black & White

High contrast scenes often shine in black and white. Try converting both versions using:

- Your camera's monochrome setting

- Basic editing software

- A phone app if shooting mobile

Notice how black & white removes the distraction of color and lets you focus on shape, shadow, and light geometry.

Take at least one photo with bold shadows or bright highlights in black & white.

Step 5: Modify or Redirect the Light (Optional)

If you're photographing a portrait or still life and want to soften the harsh midday light:

- •Hold a small diffuser or translucent white object (like a shopping bag or thin cloth) over your subject.

- •Use a reflector or white card to bounce light into the shadows.

- •Move your subject into open shade, but stay near the bright area to preserve contrast.

Take a photo with modified light and compare it to your full-sun version.

Review and Compare

Upload your images and analyze:

- •Which exposure best tells the story?

- •Do blown highlights or deep shadows help or hurt the image?

- •Does the black & white version feel more powerful?

Reflect on whether the contrast helped emphasize shape, mood, or message—and how you might use that next time.

Key Concepts to Remember

High Noon Light:

- •Tone: Cool, bright, intense

- •Quality: Hard, directional, contrasty

- •Mood: Bold, edgy, unfiltered

- •Challenges: Harsh shadows, clipped highlights, squinting subjects

- •Opportunities: Strong graphics, textures, black & white, grit

Tips for Shooting in Midday Sun:

- Look for patterns of light and dark—shadows become compositional tools

- Expose for highlights to preserve drama; expose for shadows for mood

- Use black & white to emphasize tone and shape

- Modify light only when needed—embrace the boldness

Why This Will Make Your Photos Better

Photographers who master high-contrast light become problem-solvers. You'll stop fearing "bad" lighting and start seeing potential everywhere. You'll know how to protect highlight detail when needed, how to emphasize geometry and lines, and how to creatively work with whatever the day gives you.

Most importantly, you'll learn that every type of light has a story to tell—even the hard, honest light of noon.

Quick Daily Practice

Next time you're out mid-day:

- Look for bold shadow patterns on walls, pavement, or faces.

- Photograph an ordinary object and let the shadow become part of the design.

- Ask: What does the contrast add to this moment?

Final Thought

Midday light challenges you to be thoughtful, not lucky. It forces choices, asks for control, and rewards boldness. Learn to see the structure beneath the glare—and your photographs will gain strength and presence, even in the brightest light of day.

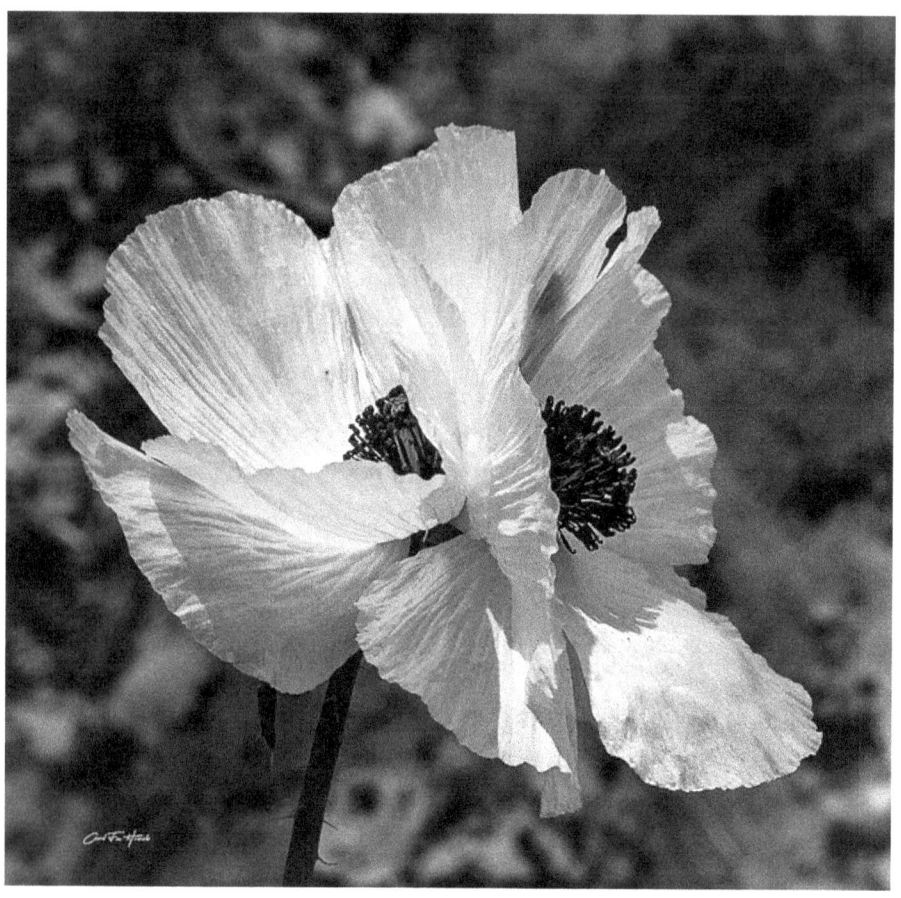

This image of a White Prickly Poppy, captured under the intense overhead sun, perfectly illustrates how harsh midday light can be used intentionally to reveal detail and drama. With the sun high in the sky, shadows fall directly beneath the flower, and the strong, directional light illuminates the delicate, crepe-like texture of the petals. Rather than avoiding this contrast, I embraced it—converting the image to black and white to further emphasize the flower's form, edges, and intricate textures. Day 6 encourages us not to fear the so-called "bad light" of midday, but to harness it for its clarity and intensity. In this photo, the hard light becomes an asset, showcasing the structure and elegance of the double bloom in a way that softer light couldn't.

Day 6 Reflective Journal Pages

Use these prompts to reflect after each lesson or at the end of each week. There's no right or wrong way to answer—let your thoughts flow honestly and creatively.

Day 6: High Noon Contrast

1. What did I observe about the light today?

2. What surprised or challenged me during this lesson?

3. Which image felt the strongest—and why?

4. What would I do differently if I repeated this exercise?

5. Notes, thoughts, or ideas sparked today:

[Space for writing or sketching]

Day 7: The Direction of Light

"Before you change your settings—change your position.
Direction changes everything."

Why This Matters

You can have the perfect exposure, beautiful color, and a compelling subject—but if the light is coming from the wrong direction, your photo can still fall flat.

The direction of light—whether it hits your subject from the front, side, back, or top—dramatically affects how we seethat subject. It defines shape, reveals or hides texture, influences mood, and determines what the viewer's eye will focus on. Once you learn to recognize and control light direction, you'll stop simply capturing scenes and start sculpting them.

Changing your perspective relative to the light is one of the simplest and most powerful tools in photography. And best of all—it doesn't cost a thing. *Just move your feet.*

What You'll Learn Today

- •The four primary directions of light and how they influence your image
- •How to position yourself or your subject for different effects
- •How to use directional light to emphasize mood, shape, and texture
- •The importance of intentional light placement in composition

Step-by-Step Exercise: One Subject, Four Directions

You'll photograph the same subject from four angles: front, side, back, and overhead light, to see how direction changes impact.

What You Need

- •DSLR or mirrorless camera
- •One simple subject (portrait, flower, sculpture, or textured object)
- •A consistent light source: window, lamp, or sunlight
- •A turntable or table where the subject can be rotated (or you move around it)
- •Optional: reflector or white board

Step 1: Front Light

Position the light source behind you, facing your subject directly.

📌 Front light is clear, even, and low in shadow.

- •Focus on the overall clarity and color of the image.
- •Observe how shadows are minimized—details may be flatter.

Take a few images. This setup is useful for documentation and bright, straightforward looks.

Step 2: Side Light

Now shift so the light hits the subject from the left or right.

📌 Side light adds depth, form, and shadow contrast.

- •Observe how one side is lit while the other falls into shadow.
- •Texture becomes more visible, and shape is emphasized.

Try a close-up shot to emphasize texture. This is ideal for moody portraits or textured still life.

Step 3: Back Light

Move so the light is behind the subject, facing into your camera.

📌 Back light creates glow, rim light, or silhouettes.

　　•Use exposure compensation to avoid underexposing your subject.

　　•Observe how the light outlines your subject's shape.

Try capturing glow through translucent areas or dramatic silhouettes for mood.

Step 4: Top Light

Place the light source directly above your subject (or shoot outside at high noon).

📌 Top light can be harsh, especially for portraits, but dramatic for shapes.

　　•Observe how shadows fall directly downward.

　　•Often used in dramatic or gritty black & white images.

Be mindful of deep shadows under eyebrows, noses, or chins—use reflectors if needed.

Step 5: Review and Compare

Place your four images side-by-side.

Ask:

　　•Which direction emphasizes texture? Shape? Mood?

　　•Which feels the most emotionally engaging?

　　•How do shadows help or hurt your image?

Write a brief note on which direction worked best for your subject and why.

Key Concepts to Remember

1. Front Light

   •Pros: Clear, bright, low shadow

   •Cons: Flat, little dimension

   •Best For: Product shots, documentation, vibrant color

2. Side Light

   •Pros: Adds depth, reveals texture

   •Cons: Can be too contrasty without fill light

   •Best For: Portraits, still life, architecture

3. Back Light

   •Pros: Creates glow, mood, rim light

   •Cons: Requires exposure compensation or fill light

   •Best For: Portraits, flowers, creative scenes

4. Top Light

   •Pros: Dramatic contrast, bold shape

   •Cons: Unflattering for faces, harsh shadows

   •Best For: Black & white, abstract, strong compositions

Why This Will Make Your Photos Better

Learning to notice and use light direction is a major shift
from taking photos to making them. You gain control over how your
subject is perceived—what is revealed, what is hidden, and what emotion
is conveyed.

Instead of defaulting to whatever light is available, you begin to ask:

•Where should the light be for this subject?

•What do I want my viewer to feel?

That intentionality is what makes you not just a camera user—but a photographer.

Quick Daily Practice

Throughout the day, choose any object nearby and:

•Walk around it to observe how light direction changes its appearance.

•Practice seeing where the shadows fall.

•Ask: Which side tells the most interesting visual story?

Under harsh sunlight, I exposed for the shadows in this side view of the Prickly Pear bloom. The light source, the sun, is above and slightly behind the flower. This view allows us to see the translucency of the petals as well as the details of the emerging thorns.

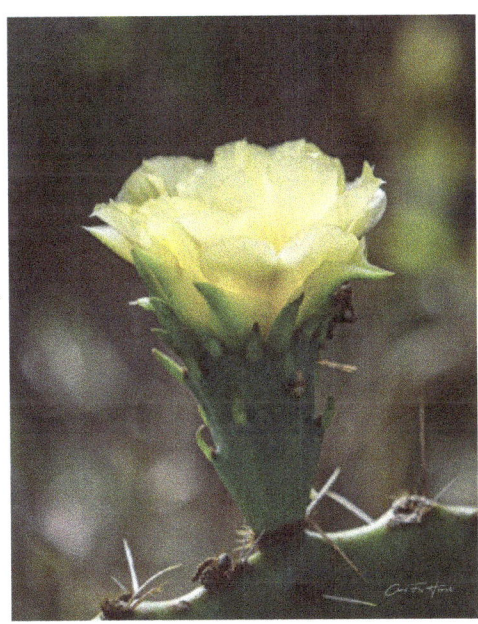

Final Thought

The light is always there. It's the way you approach it that changes the photograph. Move your body. Turn your subject. Ask more from the light, and it will give you more than you imagined.

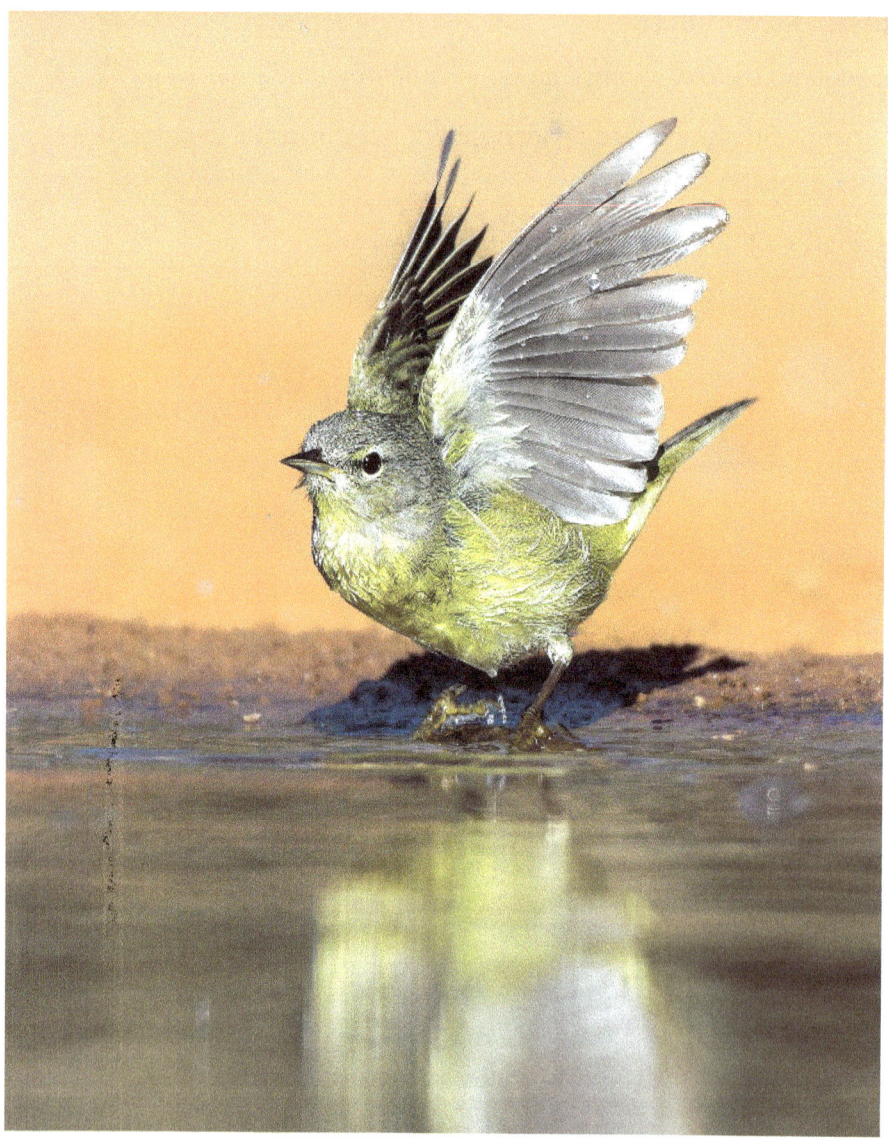

This photograph of an Orange-crowned Warbler, taken with the sun behind me and falling directly onto the bird, is a clear example of how front lighting can be used to achieve even illumination and sharp detail. With the light striking the subject head-on, the bird's features—its subtle coloring, feather patterns, and eye detail—are all clearly visible without deep shadows or harsh highlights. The water also reflects fill light onto the subject.

Day 7 focuses on the direction of light and how it affects the mood and visibility of a subject. In this case, the front light offers a clean, documentary-style rendering, perfect for showing fine detail and accurate color. This type of lighting may lack drama, but it excels at clarity—making it a strong choice for wildlife portraits like this one, where sharpness and realism are key.

Day 7 Reflective Journal Pages

Use these prompts to reflect after each lesson or at the end of each week. There's no right or wrong way to answer—let your thoughts flow honestly and creatively.

Day 7: The Direction of Light

1. What did I observe about the light today?

2. What surprised or challenged me during this lesson?

3. Which image felt the strongest—and why?

4. What would I do differently if I repeated this exercise?

5. Notes, thoughts, or ideas sparked today:

[Space for writing or sketching]

Week 1 Reflection: Observing the Light

Now that you've completed the first seven lessons, you've begun to experience what it means to see like a photographer. You've watched how light changes mood, texture, and direction—and how those qualities shape every image you make. You've stood in golden light, noticed the gentleness of open shade, and wrestled with the hard contrast of midday sun. Most importantly, you've started to build the habit of slowing down and paying attention. From here on, every lesson will build on this new way of seeing. You're no longer chasing light—you're learning to read it, understand it, and use it with intention. That's where the magic begins.

Week 2 Introduction: Exposure & Camera Settings

With a strong foundation in light awareness, Week 2 shifts into the technical heart of photography: exposure. No groans please! We dive into understanding how aperture, shutter speed, and ISO work together to capture light accurately and creatively. This week empowers us to move beyond automatic settings, gaining confidence in exposure control under various lighting scenarios.

Each day introduces a core element of exposure, with practical exercises that reveal how camera settings affect motion, depth, brightness, and contrast. Week 2 also covers tools like the histogram and metering modes, encouraging us to make informed decisions behind the lens.

By the end of this week, we will have the tools to translate what we see— and feel—into well-exposed, expressive images.

Day 8: The Exposure Triangle

> "Photography is the art of balancing light—
> and the exposure triangle is your foundation."

Why This Matters

Every photograph is built on light. And capturing that light properly—so your image is neither too dark nor too bright—relies on three fundamental settings: aperture, shutter speed, and ISO. Together, these make up the exposure triangle.

When you understand how these three settings interact, you unlock the ability to photograph with intention. You no longer rely on your camera's automatic settings. You begin to decide what should be in focus, how movement is rendered, and how clean or grainy your photo looks.

This is where photography becomes creative instead of just technical. Mastering the exposure triangle puts you in control—and it starts with today's lesson.

What You'll Learn Today

- •What aperture, shutter speed, and ISO do—and how they affect each other
- •How each setting changes the look of your photo (not just the brightness)
- •How to make exposure decisions based on your creative intent
- •How to practice balancing exposure manually

Key Concepts: What Is the Exposure Triangle?

Each side of the triangle represents one of the three exposure controls:

1. Aperture (f-stop)

   •Controls how wide the lens opens to let in light

   •Affects depth of field (how much of your image is in focus)

   •Wide aperture (f/2.8) = more light + blurry background

   •Narrow aperture (f/11, f/16) = less light + more in focus

2. Shutter Speed

   •Controls how long the shutter stays open

   •Affects motion in the image

   •Fast shutter (1/500s) = freezes motion

   •Slow shutter (1/15s) = blurs movement

3. ISO

   •Controls how sensitive the sensor is to light

   •Affects image quality

   •Low ISO (100–200) = clean, less noise

   •High ISO (1600–3200+) = brighter, but more digital grain

How They Work Together

Think of them like a triangle with a fixed size: if you change one corner (say, a wider aperture), you need to adjust at least one of the others (like faster shutter speed or lower ISO) to maintain balance.

This balance is the key to correct exposure—and to creative control.

Step-by-Step Exercise: Balancing the Triangle

Today, you'll photograph a still subject using Manual Mode and adjust the triangle to maintain correct exposure while creatively changing the image's look.

What You Need

- •DSLR or mirrorless camera with Manual mode (M)
- •A lens with a large aperture range.
- •A still subject (book, vase, plant, etc.) near a window or lamp
- •A notepad or app to track your settings
- •Tripod or steady surface (optional)

Step 1: Set a Baseline Exposure

- •Choose a midday or well-lit indoor spot.
- •Set ISO to 200 (for low noise).
- •Choose f/5.6 and shutter speed of 1/125s.
- •Take a test photo.

If the image is too dark or bright:

- •Adjust one setting until the light meter inside the viewfinder reads "0" (neutral exposure).
- •Write down your three settings: aperture – shutter speed – ISO.

This is your baseline exposure.

Step 2: Change the Aperture

Now widen the aperture (e.g., from f/5.6 to f/2.8) to make the opening larger.

- •Notice: More light enters, and the background becomes blurrier.

- •To maintain exposure, increase shutter speed (make it faster).
- •Take a photo and compare to your baseline.

Now try narrowing the aperture (e.g., to f/11 or f/16) to make the opening smaller.

- •Less light enters; more is in focus.
- •Compensate by slowing shutter speed (e.g., from 1/125s to 1/30s).
- •Take another photo.

Observe how depth of field changes with aperture.

Step 3: Change the Shutter Speed

Return to baseline settings. Now experiment with shutter speed.

- •Try a faster shutter (e.g., 1/500s).
- •Compensate by widening the aperture or increasing ISO.
- •Then try a slower shutter (e.g., 1/15s) and do the same.

Take notes on how motion and brightness are affected.

Step 4: Change the ISO

Start again with baseline settings.

- •Increase ISO to 800 or 1600.
- •Notice how brightness increases.
- •Adjust shutter speed or aperture to maintain balance.

Take a close look at the image for digital noise or grain.

Step 5: Review and Reflect

Compare all your photos:

- •Which setting combinations gave you the look you liked most?
- •Where did you lose quality? Where did you gain creative control?

•How did adjusting one setting require you to think about the others?

Write a summary of what you learned about balancing exposure for both technical accuracy and creative effect.

Why This Will Make Your Photos Better

Understanding the exposure triangle is your gateway to creative freedom. You'll no longer be guessing or relying on Auto mode. You'll be able to make purposeful decisions:

•Blurry background or all in focus? → Aperture

•Freeze action or show motion? → Shutter Speed

•Clean image or brighter exposure? → ISO

It's the difference between hoping for a good photo and knowing how to create one.

Quick Daily Practice

•Pick one scene, then take three photos:

1. Aperture priority (wide open)
2. Shutter priority (fast)
3. Manual mode (balanced exposure)

•Compare how they feel—and how your triangle shifted.

Final Thought

Once you master this triangle, photography feels less like a puzzle and more like a playground. You'll begin to see light not as a challenge—but as a set of choices you know how to balance with skill and creativity.

ISO 400•1/1250 sec•f/7.1

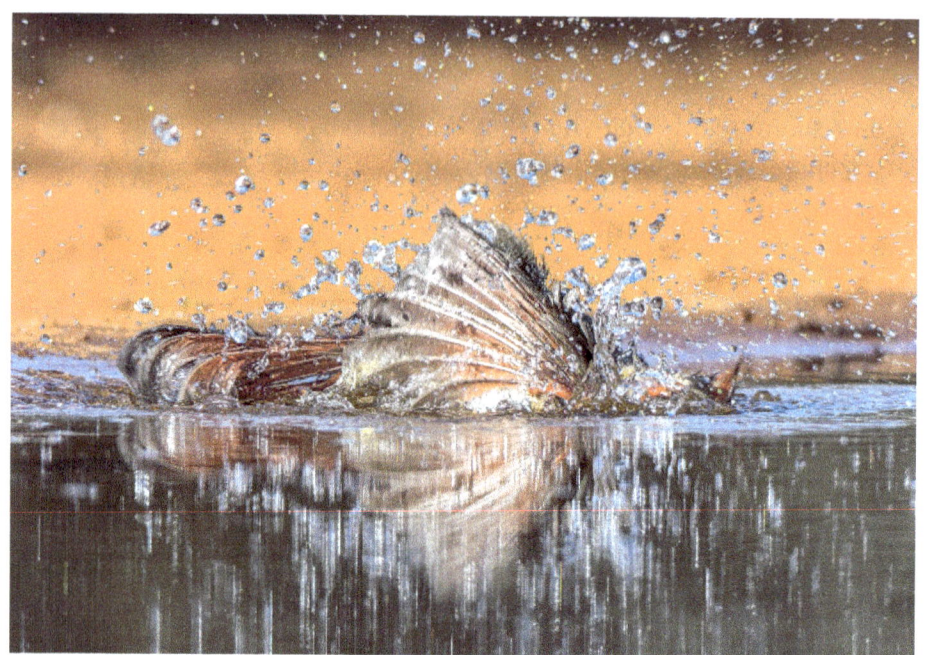

This image of a female cardinal mid-bath, caught the energetic splash of water droplets, beautifully demonstrates the importance of mastering the exposure triangle—the balance between shutter speed, aperture, and ISO. To freeze the motion of the splashing water and capture the fine detail in the feathers, I needed a fast shutter speed, which required adjusting aperture and ISO accordingly.

Day 8 teaches us how each exposure setting works in harmony: a wide aperture allowed in more light, and a higher ISO helped compensate for the speed, ensuring the image remained sharp and well-exposed. In this moment of motion, the exposure triangle wasn't just a technical necessity—it was the key to turning a fleeting action into a crisp, expressive photograph. Knowing that birds were coming into this pond to bathe each morning, I chose a fast shutter speed (1/1250 of a second) which allowed me to freeze the water droplets in mid-air but it wasn't quite fast enough to freeze the wings—there is still some motion blur, which I think helps tell the story.

Day 8 Reflective Journal Pages

Use these prompts to reflect after each lesson or at the end of each week. There's no right or wrong way to answer—let your thoughts flow honestly and creatively.

Day 8: The Exposure Triangle

1. What did I observe about the light today?

2. What surprised or challenged me during this lesson?

3. Which image felt the strongest—and why?

4. What would I do differently if I repeated this exercise?

5. Notes, thoughts, or ideas sparked today:

[Space for writing or sketching]

Day 9: Aperture and Depth of Field

"Your aperture doesn't just control light—it shapes how your viewer sees the world."

Why This Matters

Aperture is one of the most expressive tools in photography. It controls how much light enters your camera—but more importantly, it determines depth of field: the range of the image that appears in sharp focus.

Want a creamy, blurred background in a portrait? That's a wide aperture. Want a sweeping landscape where everything is sharp from foreground to background? That's a narrow aperture.

Understanding aperture allows you to direct your viewer's attention, isolate your subject, or tell a story through selective focus. It's where technical control meets artistic style.

What You'll Learn Today

- •How to control aperture using f-stops
- •What depth of field is and how it impacts your images
- •How subject distance and lens choice affect background blur
- •How to use aperture creatively to enhance your composition

Key Concepts: Understanding Aperture and f-stops

Aperture refers to the size of the opening in your lens that lets light through. It's measured in f-stops:

- •Wide apertures: f/1.8, f/2.8 → more light, shallow depth of field

- Mid-range: f/4, f/5.6 → balanced exposure, moderate depth of field

- Narrow apertures: f/11, f/16 → less light, deep depth of field

Important: Smaller f-numbers = wider opening. (Yes, it's backwards—but remember it's a fraction: f/2 is larger than f/8.)

Step-by-Step Exercise: Depth of Field in Action

Today, you'll shoot a subject at multiple aperture settings and observe how background blur and focus range change.

What You Need

- DSLR or mirrorless camera with Aperture Priority mode (A or Av)
- A lens that opens to at least f/2.8 or f/4 (a kit lens is fine)
- A subject with a clear background (e.g., flower, figurine, bottle)
- A background with some visual elements (e.g., trees, bookshelf, sidewalk)

Step 1: Set Up Your Subject

Place your subject on a table, ledge, or in an outdoor setting with space between the subject and the background.

📌 The more space between subject and background, the more blur you'll see with wide apertures.

Step 2: Shoot Wide Open (Shallow Depth of Field)

- Set your camera to Aperture Priority mode
- Choose the lowest f-stop your lens allows (e.g., f/2.8, f/3.5)
- Focus on your subject's nearest detail (eye, edge, center)

Take a photo and observe:

- Subject in sharp focus

•Background soft or fully blurred

•This is ideal for portraits, detail shots, and isolating a subject

Step 3: Stop Down (Increase Depth of Field)

Change your aperture to f/5.6 and take another photo. Then try f/11 or f/16.

•Notice how more of the scene comes into focus

•Background elements become more defined

•Subject may blend in more, depending on distance

Take 2–3 shots at different f-stops for comparison.

Step 4: Move and Repeat

Now try moving closer to your subject and repeat the shots.

📌 Closer subject = shallower depth of field at the same aperture

Also try stepping back and using a longer focal length if possible (zoom in). This will further compress the background and exaggerate blur with a wide aperture.

Step 5: Review and Compare

Load your images and compare them side-by-side.

Ask:

•How much of the background stayed in focus at each setting?

•Which version draws your eye more quickly to the subject?

•How does the change in aperture affect the mood or message?

■ Make note of which f-stop worked best for your subject—and how distance and focal length impacted the result.

Key Concepts to Remember

Shallow Depth of Field

- Aperture: f/1.8 to f/4

- Look: Soft background (bokeh), subject pops

- Best For: Portraits, detail shots, isolating a subject

- Tips: Increase distance between subject and background; move closer

Deep Depth of Field

- Aperture: f/8 to f/16

- Look: Entire scene in focus

- Best For: Landscapes, architecture, group shots

- Tips: Use tripod for low-light situations at narrow apertures

Why This Will Make Your Photos Better

Aperture gives you power over storytelling. You choose whether your viewer sees only the subject—or the whole scene. Whether a photo feels intimate and focused, or expansive and detailed. This kind of control adds professionalism and intent to your photography.

And once you've mastered aperture, you'll be able to answer the most important question behind every great image:
"What do I want people to see—and feel—first?"

Quick Daily Practice

- •Choose a subject and photograph it at f/2.8, f/5.6, and f/11
- •Move closer, then farther away
- •Try zooming in (if using a zoom lens)
- •Study how depth of field shifts in each version

ISO 250•1/160 sec•f/22

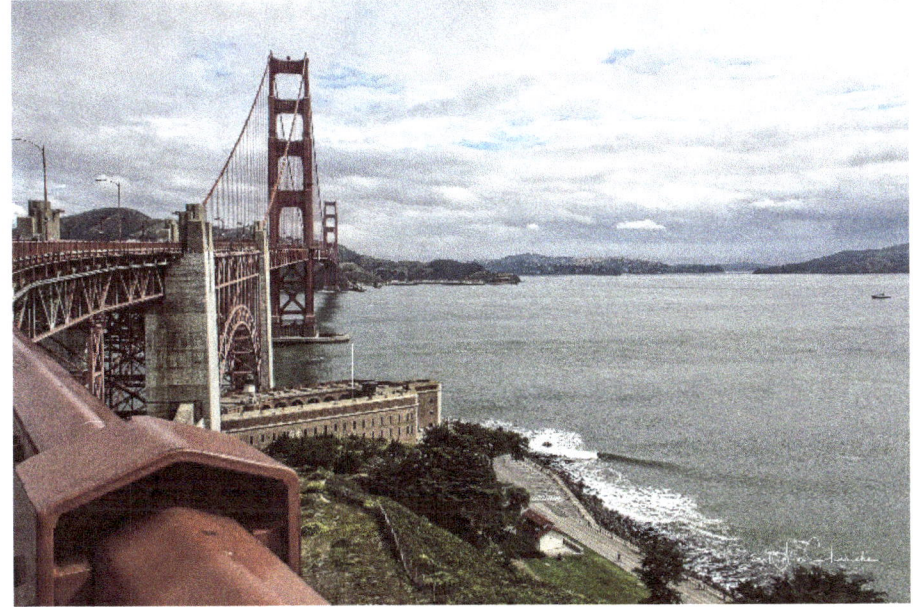

Using an aperture of f/22 allowed me to have the entire Golden Gate Bridge in focus.

Final Thought

Depth of field is one of the most expressive tools in photography. Learn to control it, and you'll start shaping not just your exposures—but your viewer's experience of the image.

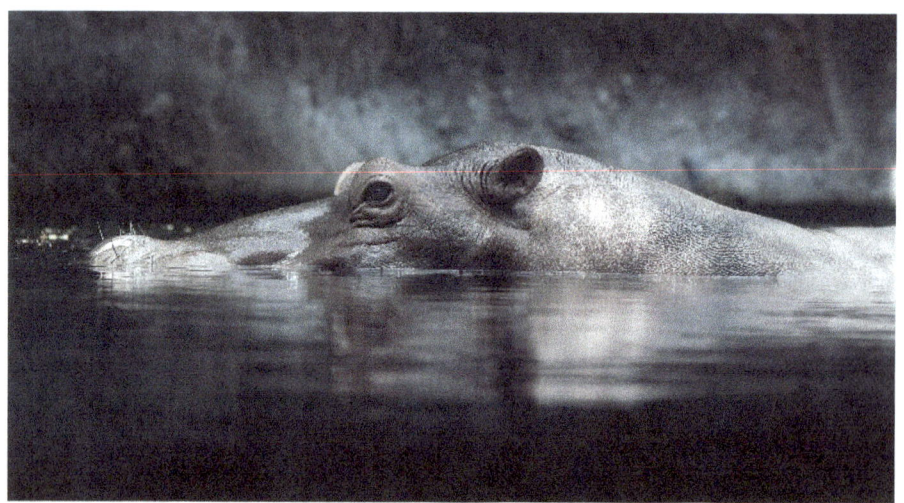

ISO 400•1/320 sec•f/5.0

This image of a rhinoceros partially submerged in water showcases how aperture choice directly affects depth of field and visual storytelling. By using a wide aperture, I was able to isolate the rhino from its surroundings, creating a beautifully blurred foreground and background while keeping the subject in sharp focus. This draws the viewer's attention immediately to the texture of the rhino's skin and the stillness of the water around it, while the softened elements add a sense of atmosphere and depth. Day 9 emphasizes how aperture controls more than just exposure—it shapes the mood and focus of the frame. In this image, shallow depth of field transforms a documentary-style moment into a more intimate and artistic portrait of a powerful animal in a moment of calm.

Day 9 Reflective Journal Pages

Use these prompts to reflect after each lesson or at the end of each week. There's no right or wrong way to answer—let your thoughts flow honestly and creatively.

Day 9: Aperture and Depth of Field

6. What did I observe about the light today?

7. What surprised or challenged me during this lesson?

8. Which image felt the strongest—and why?

9. What would I do differently if I repeated this exercise?

10. Notes, thoughts, or ideas sparked today:

[Space for writing or sketching]

Day 10: Freezing and Blurring Motion

"Time is a choice in photography—
you can stop it cold or let it flow."

Why This Matters

One of the most powerful—and often underused—tools in photography
is shutter speed. It not only controls how much light hits your sensor, but
it also determines how motion appears in your images.

Do you want to freeze a bird in mid-flight, sharp and crisp? Or do you
want to blur a waterfall so it looks like smooth silk? Shutter speed makes
both possible. When you learn to control it, you gain the ability to
add energy, calm, drama, or elegance to your photos—just by deciding
how you capture movement.

Today's exercise helps you explore both ends of the spectrum: freezing
action and embracing blur.

What You'll Learn Today

- How shutter speed affects motion in your photos
- How to freeze fast movement with high shutter speeds
- How to blur motion creatively with slow shutter speeds
- How to use camera settings to support each choice

Key Concepts: What is Shutter Speed?

Shutter speed refers to how long the shutter stays open to let light reach
the sensor. It's measured in fractions of a second (like 1/1000s) or in
whole seconds (like 1s or 2s).

- Fast shutter speeds (1/500s – 1/4000s): Freeze action
- Slow shutter speeds (1/30s – 2s or longer): Blur motion

- Medium speeds (1/125s – 1/250s): Good for general handheld shooting

Slower speeds often require a tripod or steady hand to prevent camera shake.

Step-by-Step Exercise: Motion at Two Speeds

Today, you'll photograph the same moving subject twice: once to freeze it and once to blur it—learning how your choice of shutter speed affects the result.

What You Need

- DSLR or mirrorless camera with Shutter Priority mode (S or Tv) or Manual

- A moving subject: water fountain, passing car, pet, runner, waving flag, etc.

- Well-lit environment (outdoors preferred)

- Optional: Tripod or stable surface

Step 1: Freeze the Motion

Set your camera to:

- Shutter speed: Start with 1/500s or faster

- ISO: Auto or 400–800 depending on light

- Mode: Shutter Priority (S or Tv)

Find a subject in motion—kids playing, leaves blowing, traffic moving, someone jumping—and take several shots.

Observe:

- Is the movement perfectly sharp or still slightly blurred?

•Do you like the sense of stillness and frozen time?

Now try increasing your shutter speed to 1/1000s or 1/2000s, especially for faster subjects (like birds, running dogs, or splashing water).

Note how freezing motion often increases sharpness and visual impact.

Step 2: Blur the Motion

Now slow the shutter speed to 1/30s, 1/15s, or even 1 second.

•You may need to lower ISO or use a smaller aperture (like f/11 or f/16) to avoid overexposure.

•Use a tripod or place your camera on something stable.

•Focus on a subject that moves smoothly—like water, people walking, flags blowing, or spinning wheels.

Try panning: follow a moving subject (like a cyclist or runner) with your camera while using 1/30s or slower. The subject may stay sharp while the background blurs.

Observe:

•Does the blur feel artistic? Dreamy? Chaotic?

•Are you suggesting motion, rhythm, energy?

Step 3: Review and Compare

Look at your freezing vs. blurring images.

Ask:

•Which one tells a stronger story?

•Which feels more energetic or more peaceful?

•Was it harder to control exposure or focus in either case?

Write down the shutter speeds you found most effective—and what subject types work best for each style.

Key Concepts to Remember

To Freeze Motion

- •Use shutter speeds 1/500s or faster

- •Raise ISO or widen aperture to keep exposure balanced

- •Works best in bright light or with fast lenses

- •Ideal for: Sports, wildlife, street, splash photography

To Blur Motion

- •Use 1/30s or slower

- •Use a tripod or stable support

- •Can blur entire frame or just the moving parts

- •Ideal for: Waterfalls, light trails, panning shots, artistic motion blur

Why This Will Make Your Photos Better

Mastering shutter speed lets you shape time in your images. You can stop a fleeting moment with crystal clarity—or let the movement unfold to express mood or flow. It's no longer about what's happening— but how you choose to show it.

Whether you're photographing dance, rushing water, or falling leaves, your control over motion makes your work feel intentional and professional.

Quick Daily Practice

- •Choose one subject in motion and photograph it at:

  - •1/1000s (frozen)
  - •1/125s (natural)
  - •1/15s or 1s (blurred)

•Reflect: Which one communicates more emotion? Which one surprised you?

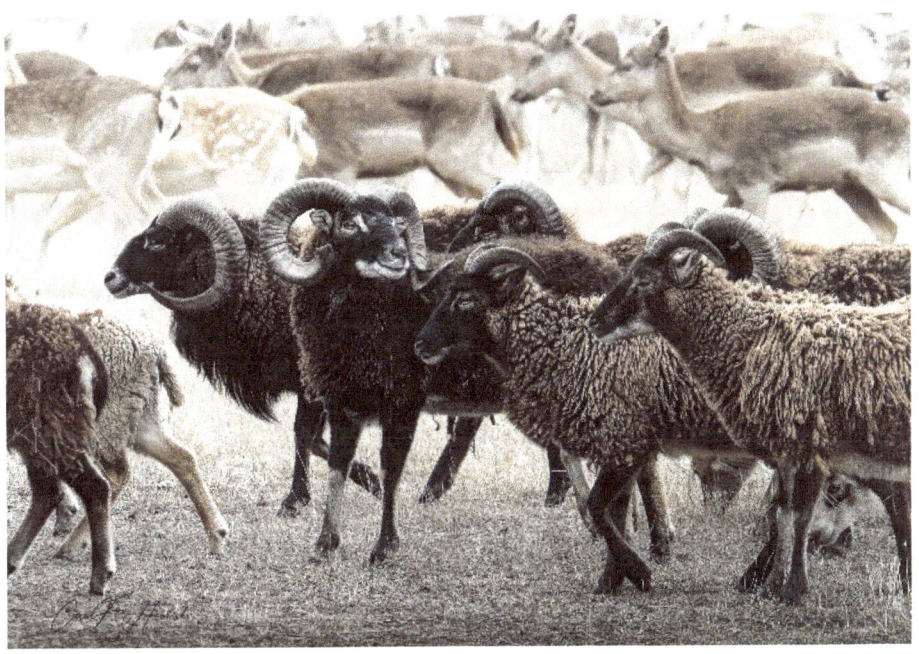

1/1250 sec was fast enough to freeze the movement of the deer and sheep.

Final Thought

Photography lets you control time—and once you realize that, your storytelling becomes deeper and more personal. Whether you're freezing someone mid-jump or blurring rain across a windshield, remember you're no longer just taking a picture. You're capturing a moment the way you want it to be remembered.

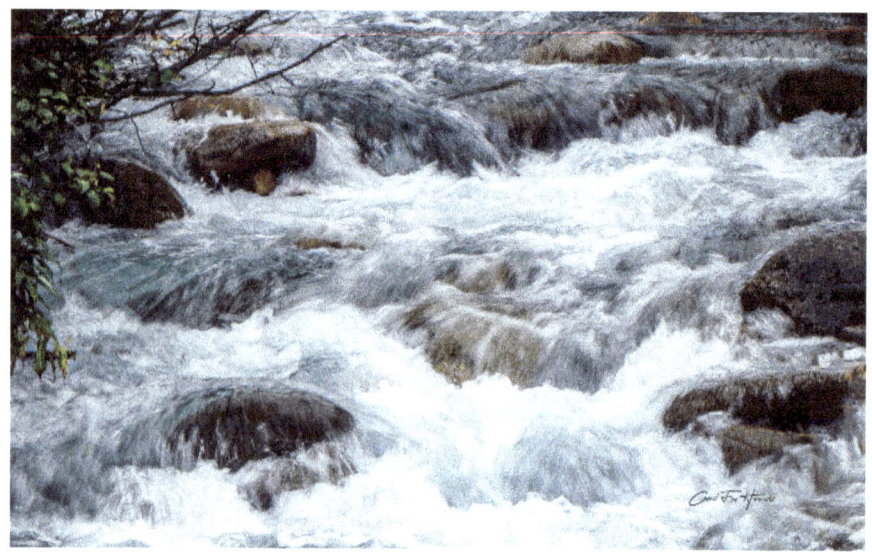

This photograph of a rushing creek, with water spilling over rocks and captured at a slow shutter speed, beautifully illustrates the concept of motion blur explored in Day 10. Rather than freezing each droplet, I intentionally slowed the shutter to allow the movement of the water to become a soft, flowing blur—creating a sense of motion, rhythm, and serenity. The surrounding rocks remain sharp, grounding the image and enhancing the visual contrast between stillness and motion. This lesson is about using shutter speed not just to control exposure, but to shape the feeling of a scene. In this image, blurring the water conveys the continuous, graceful energy of the creek—turning a fleeting moment into something timeless and expressive.

Day 10 Reflective Journal Pages

Use these prompts to reflect after each lesson or at the end of each week. There's no right or wrong way to answer—let your thoughts flow honestly and creatively.

Day 10: Freezing and Blurring Motion

1. What did I observe about the light today?

2. What surprised or challenged me during this lesson?

3. Which image felt the strongest—and why?

4. What would I do differently if I repeated this exercise?

5. Notes, thoughts, or ideas sparked today:

[Space for writing or sketching]

Day 11: Low Light Mastery

"Low light doesn't mean no light—it means new possibilities."

Why This Matters

Low-light situations are where many beginner photographers struggle—and where many professionals shine. Whether you're indoors at dusk, photographing city lights at night, or capturing the quiet glow of candlelight, understanding how to handle low light is essential to becoming a confident, capable photographer.

Instead of seeing low light as a limitation, this lesson helps you see it as a creative opportunity. It's in the shadows and subtle tones that stories deepen and mood emerges. With the right techniques and camera settings, you'll not only managelow light—you'll master it.

What You'll Learn Today

- How to adjust your camera settings for low-light conditions
- How to prevent blurry images without using flash
- How ISO, aperture, and shutter speed work together in dim light
- How to embrace low light creatively for emotion, texture, and atmosphere

Key Concepts: What is Low Light?

Low light doesn't mean total darkness. It refers to any situation where your scene is:

- Indoors with limited window or artificial light
- Outdoors at dawn, dusk, or nighttime

•Shaded or overcast with heavy cloud cover

These environments can be rich with emotion, but require thoughtful exposure.

Step-by-Step Exercise: Shooting in Low Light

You'll photograph a still subject in a dim or low-light environment using different settings to explore what works—and what doesn't.

What You Need

- •DSLR or mirrorless camera

- •A subject in a dimly lit room (lamp, candle, or window light works well)

- •Tripod or flat surface (optional but helpful)

- •Manual or Aperture Priority mode

Step 1: Widen the Aperture

Start by selecting Aperture Priority mode (A or Av).

- •Choose your lowest f-stop (e.g., f/1.8 to f/3.5).

- •This allows more light to hit the sensor.

- •The tradeoff: shallower depth of field—be mindful of focus.

Take a few shots and note the exposure time your camera selects.

Step 2: Raise the ISO

Now experiment with ISO.

- •Start at ISO 400 and increase incrementally (ISO 800, 1600, 3200).

- •As ISO increases, your camera becomes more sensitive to light.

•The tradeoff: higher ISO introduces digital noise (grain).

Take one image at each ISO level. Zoom in later to see where noise becomes distracting.

Step 3: Slow Down the Shutter Speed

Now switch to Manual mode or use a tripod with Aperture Priority.

•Try shutter speeds from 1/30s down to 1 second.

•For speeds slower than 1/60s, use a tripod or place your camera on a flat surface to avoid blur.

•Use a 2-second self-timer to prevent camera shake when pressing the shutter.

This technique is great for low-light landscapes, candlelit still life, or moody scenes.

Step 4: Add or Modify the Light (Optional)

If you want a cleaner image without using high ISO:

•Add a lamp, phone light, or flashlight off to the side.

•Reflect light back using a white card or piece of paper.

•Use curtains or diffusers to soften the added light.

Take a photo before and after adding light. Compare the sharpness, color, and noise.

Step 5: Review and Compare

Look at your series of images and evaluate:

•Which exposure settings gave you the cleanest results?

•Where does noise start to affect quality?

•Does the mood feel more intimate, dramatic, or mysterious in low light?

•Which image feels most emotionally engaging?

Make notes on what worked and what to watch out for next time.

Key Concepts to Remember

Low Light Shooting Tips

- Aperture: Use the widest your lens allows (f/1.8–f/3.5)

- Shutter Speed: Keep above 1/60s handheld—or use a tripod for slower speeds

- ISO: Don't be afraid to go higher—but test your camera's limits

- Stabilization: Use a tripod or brace your camera to avoid blur

- Focus Manually: In very dim light, autofocus can struggle— switch to manual if needed

Why This Will Make Your Photos Better

Once you master low light, you'll stop putting your camera away when the sun goes down. You'll be able to photograph candlelit dinners, city streets at night, glowing storefronts, misty mornings, and quiet interiors. And you'll discover that mood lives in the shadows—not just in the highlights.

Low-light scenes have a quiet drama all their own. The glow of a lamp, the reflection of streetlights on wet pavement, the warm shadows at dusk —they all tell stories that bright daylight can't.

Quick Daily Practice

- Choose one indoor scene and photograph it at:

  - ISO 400, f/2.8, 1/60s

  - ISO 1600, f/2.8, 1/125s

  - ISO 100, f/2.8, 1s (on tripod)

•Compare for noise, sharpness, and mood

ISO 640•1/100 sec•f/10

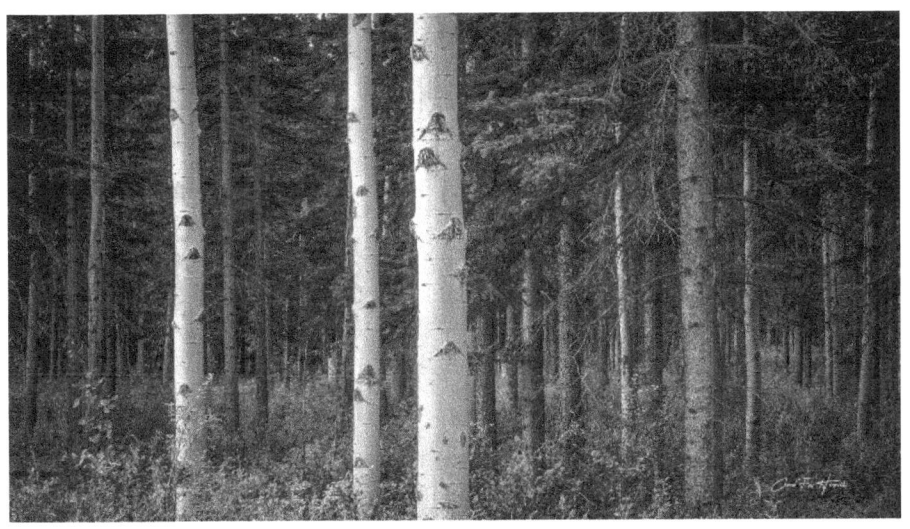

Final Thought

Light doesn't have to be bright to be beautiful. In fact, some of the most moving photographs are made when light is barely there. Learn to embrace the shadows, and you'll discover a whole new world of photographic storytelling.

The following image, captured beneath Pleasure Pier as waves rolled in at sunset, is a strong example of low light mastery in action. As the sun dropped toward the horizon, the available light faded—but instead of reaching for flash, I relied on a careful balance of aperture, shutter speed, and ISO to capture the scene naturally. The deep shadows under the pier contrasted beautifully with the warm glow reflecting off the water, creating a moody, atmospheric frame. Day 11 teaches us how to work confidently in challenging light—adjusting exposure to preserve both detail and feeling. In this photo, I embraced the low light to highlight the texture of the waves, footprints in the sand and the angular components of the structure, and the quiet drama of dusk without losing the essence of the scene.

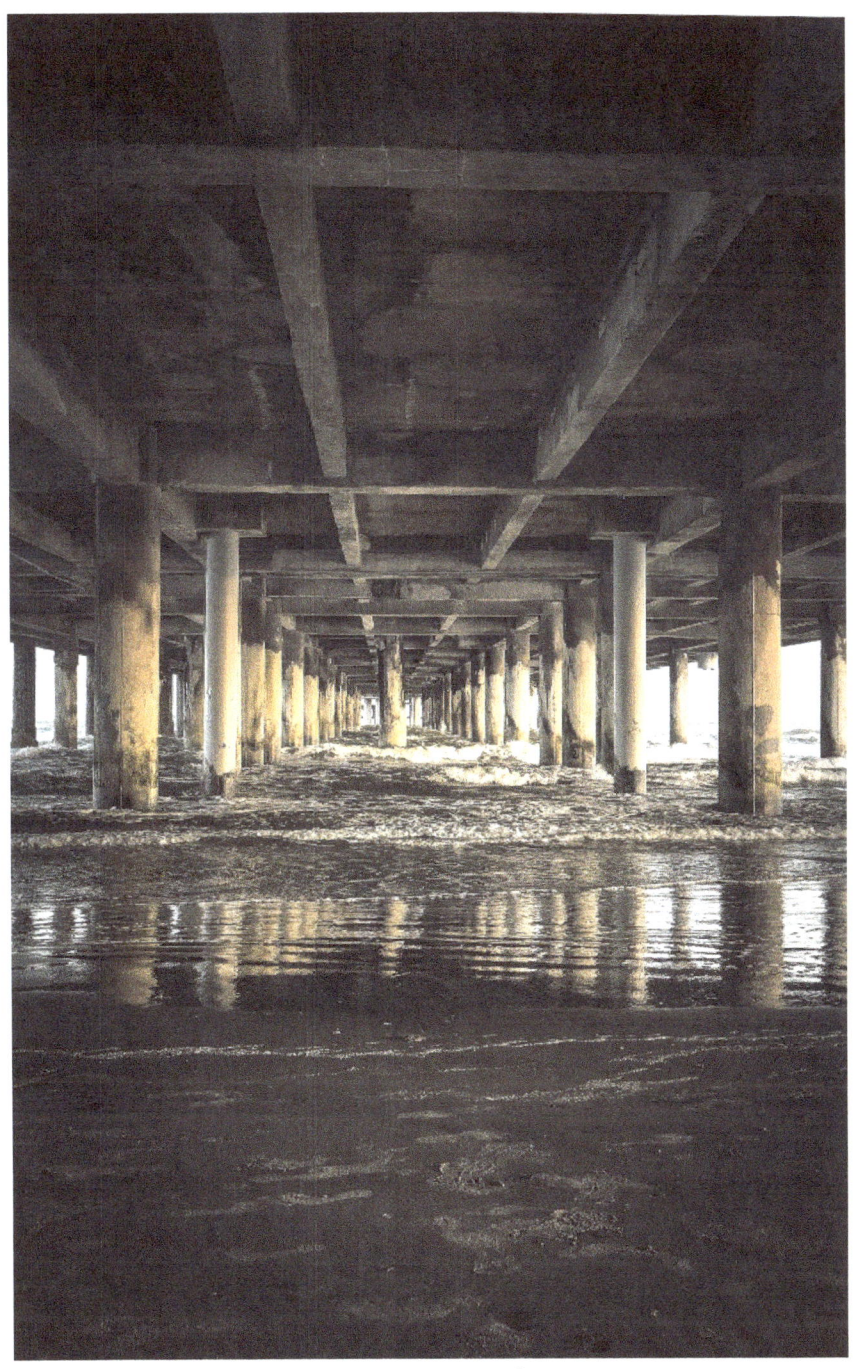

ISO 800•1/80 sec•f/3.2

Day 11 Reflective Journal Pages

Use these prompts to reflect after each lesson or at the end of each week. There's no right or wrong way to answer—let your thoughts flow honestly and creatively.

Day 11: Low Light Mastery

1. What did I observe about the light today?

2. What surprised or challenged me during this lesson?

3. Which image felt the strongest—and why?

4. What would I do differently if I repeated this exercise?

5. Notes, thoughts, or ideas sparked today:

[Space for writing or sketching]

Day 12: Histogram Check

> "Your eyes can be fooled. The histogram never lies."

Why This Matters

When you're working in varied lighting conditions—especially high contrast, low light, or bright backlight—your camera's LCD screen can be misleading. What looks perfect on the back of the camera might be too dark or blown out once you upload it.

That's where the histogram comes in. It's your secret weapon for checking exposure objectively. Instead of guessing if a photo is too bright or too dark, you can glance at this simple graph and know for sure.

Learning to read a histogram will make you more confident in your exposures and help you avoid mistakes like crushed shadows or blown highlights—before they ruin an otherwise great shot.

What You'll Learn Today

- What a histogram is and how to interpret it
- How to use it to evaluate exposure in real-time
- What common histogram shapes reveal about your image
- How to use it to fix overexposure or underexposure quickly

Key Concepts: What Is a Histogram?

A histogram is a graph that shows the brightness levels in your image.

- •The left side represents blacks and shadows
- •The middle represents midtones
- •The right side represents highlights and whites

Each section of the graph shows how many pixels fall into that tonal range.

📌 Think of it like this:

Graph Area	Tone	What It Means
Left	Shadows	Dark parts of the image
Middle	Midtones	Most natural light levels
Right	Highlights	Brightest parts of the image

Step-by-Step Exercise: Reading and Using a Histogram

Today, you'll take three photos with different exposures and use the histogram to evaluate and adjust them.

What You Need

- •DSLR or mirrorless camera
- •LCD with histogram display (enable it in settings if it's not visible)
- •One subject with both light and dark areas (e.g., a person in a shaded spot, a still life near a bright window, or a landscape scene)
- •Set camera to Aperture Priority or Manual mode

Step 1: Take a Base Photo

•Set your camera to Aperture Priority and compose your shot.

•Use no exposure compensation.

•Take a photo and then press Playback + Info to view the histogram.

Observe the graph:

•Is it pushed far to the left? (Underexposed)

•Is it crammed to the right? (Overexposed)

•Is it clipped at either edge? (Lost detail in shadows/highlights)

Underexposed with clipping in dark areas

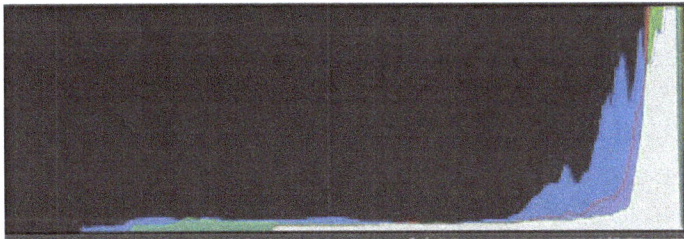

Overexposed with clipping in highlights/whites

Step 2: Underexpose Intentionally

•Set your exposure compensation to -2 stops.

•Take another photo.

Histogram will shift left: Shadows dominate, and you may lose detail in the dark areas. This might be useful for dramatic silhouettes or moody scenes.

Step 3: Overexpose Intentionally

- Set your exposure compensation to +2 stops.

- Take a photo.

Histogram will shift right: The image will look bright, and highlight areas may be lost (blown out). This might be okay for high-key images—but not for important detail like skin or sky.

Step 4: Analyze and Adjust

Now that you've seen how the histogram responds to exposure:

- Take a balanced exposure with a histogram that's spread across the middle third of the graph.

- If you're in a high-contrast scene, your histogram might not reach both ends—and that's okay if no clipping occurs.

- Watch for flat lines at either edge—this means you've lost detail there.

Note how the image looked vs. what the histogram told you. Did the image appear okay but show clipped highlights? Were you surprised by lost detail?

Understanding Histogram Shapes

Histogram Shape	What It Suggests
Bunched Left	Underexposed, dark image
Bunched Right	Overexposed, blown-out highlights
Clipped Left Edge	Lost shadow detail
Clipped Right Edge	Lost highlight detail
Even Curve Across	Balanced exposure
Peaks in Middle	Low contrast (flat)
Twin Peaks (Left & Right)	High contrast, extreme lights/darks

Why This Will Make Your Photos Better

The histogram helps you catch exposure problems in the moment—so you can fix them before moving on. It keeps you from being fooled by your screen brightness or outdoor glare. And once you trust it, you'll shoot faster, edit smarter, and waste less time wondering why a photo didn't turn out.

Whether you're protecting skin tones in a portrait or ensuring your landscape has detail in the sky, the histogram gives you the confidence that you're nailing the shot technically—while still staying creative.

Quick Daily Practice

•Take 5 photos today in various lighting conditions.

•Check the histogram for each one.

•Identify if it's underexposed, overexposed, or balanced.

•Try adjusting exposure until the histogram spreads evenly—then decide if you prefer that version.

There are absolutely times when clipping in the highlights or shadows is not only acceptable but intentional. While many photographers aim to preserve full tonal range, deliberate clipping can be a creative or stylistic choice, depending on your goals. Here's when it can be justified—or even preferred:

When Clipping Can Be Acceptable or Intentional

1. For Creative Effect or Mood

•Silhouettes: You want the shadows to clip to pure black to emphasize shape and mystery.

•High-key images: Intentionally blown-out highlights can create a soft, airy, or minimalist feel.

•Low-key images: Deep, clipped shadows can add drama, isolation, or mood.

2. To Emphasize Subject or Contrast

•Clipping less-important areas (e.g., background shadows or sky highlights) can draw attention to your subject.

•Sometimes a little clipping helps focus the viewer's eye by simplifying distractions.

3. In Harsh Lighting Conditions

•Midday sun, stage lights, or backlighting can create unavoidable clipping. If the main subject is exposed correctly and the clipped area doesn't hold critical detail, it's usually fine.

4. When Printing for Impact

•Blacks that are almost black can print muddy. Letting them go full black (clipping slightly) can make prints look punchier.

•Similarly, a bit of clipped white can add contrast in high-gloss or metal prints.

When to Be Cautious

•If you're losing important detail—like skin texture, eyes, or highlight detail in a dress or cloud—clipping can hurt the image.

•If you plan to edit heavily later, retaining full dynamic range is safer.

•If you're shooting for clients, competitions, or publications, clean histograms are often expected.

My Advice as a Photographer and Teacher

Don't fear the histogram—but don't be ruled by it either. Learn the rules, then break them with purpose. If the emotion, story, or graphic impact is stronger with a bit of clipping, and it's a conscious choice—not a mistake—you're still in creative control.

I intentionally exposed this Mexican Hat flower in order to blow out the highlights for a dreamy effect.

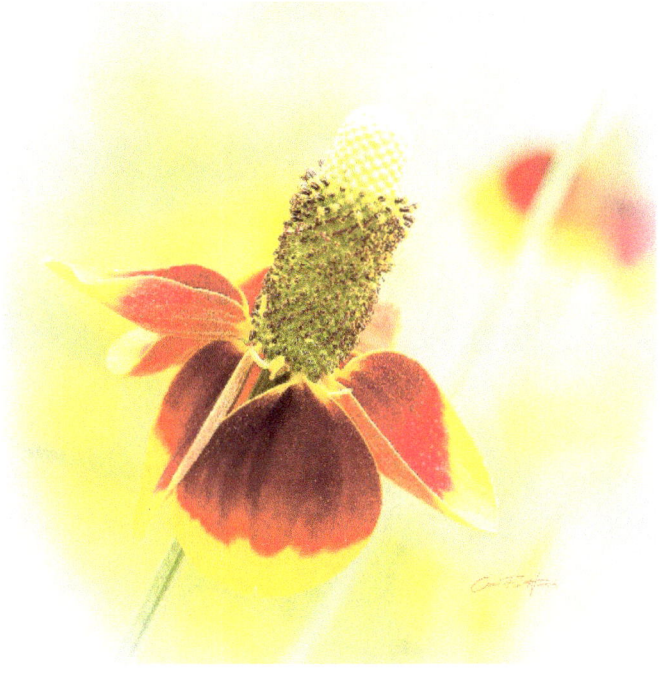

Final Thought

The histogram isn't just a technical tool—it's a truth-teller. Once you learn to read its story, you'll start seeing your light and shadow more clearly, both in-camera and in your mind's eye. And that's when photography becomes not just instinctive—but intentional.

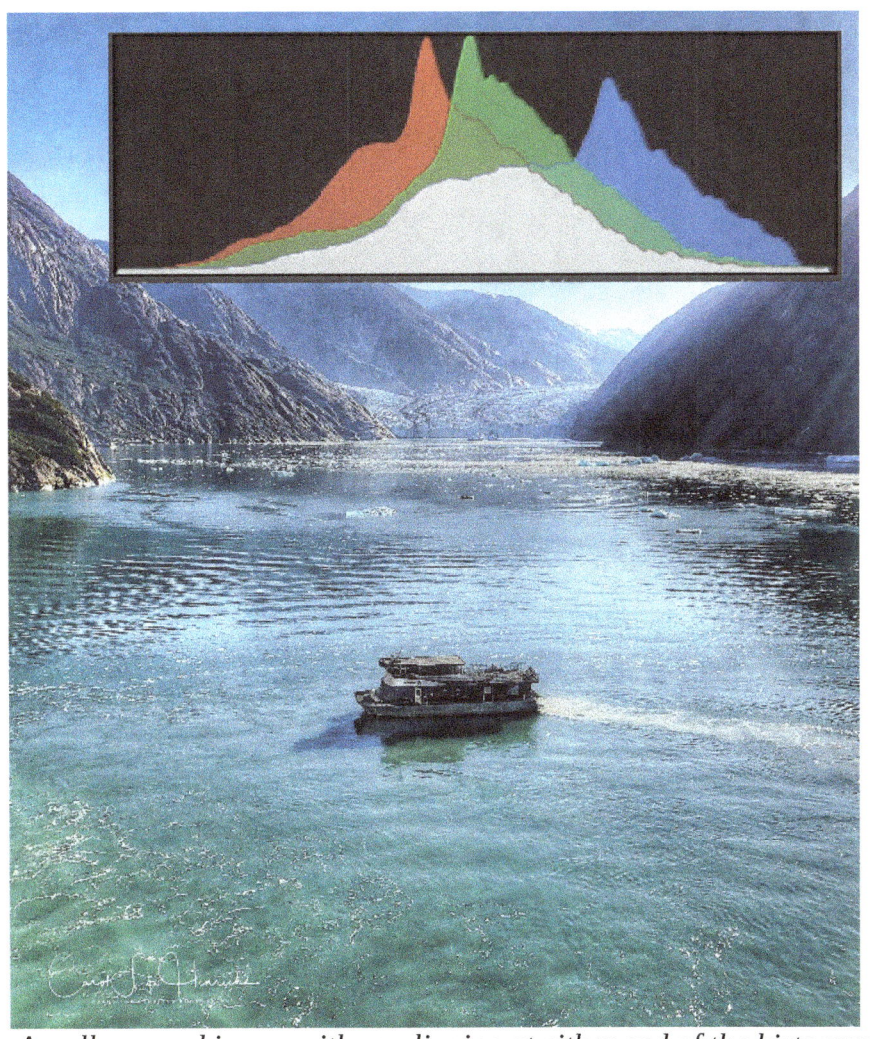

A well exposed image with no clipping at either end of the histogram

Day 12 Reflective Journal Pages

Use these prompts to reflect after each lesson or at the end of each week. There's no right or wrong way to answer—let your thoughts flow honestly and creatively.

Day 12: Histogram Check

1. What did I observe about the light today?

2. What surprised or challenged me during this lesson?

3. Which image felt the strongest—and why?

4. What would I do differently if I repeated this exercise?

5. Notes, thoughts, or ideas sparked today:

[Space for writing or sketching]

Day 13: Exposure Bracketing

"Sometimes, the best exposure isn't a single image

—it's a thoughtful blend of light and shadow."

Why This Matters

Even when you're confident with your exposure settings, some scenes are just too challenging for a single perfect shot. Think of a bright sky with a shadowed foreground, a person standing against a glowing window, or a sunbeam slicing through a dark forest. These are high dynamic range scenes—situations where the camera can't capture both highlight and shadow detail in one frame.

Enter exposure bracketing. This technique lets you take multiple images of the same scene at different exposures—usually one underexposed, one normal, and one overexposed—so you can either choose the best version later or combine them into one well-balanced photo using post-processing.

Bracketing is especially helpful when shooting landscapes, architecture, or any time you're working in contrast-heavy environments where preserving detail across the whole tonal range matters.

What You'll Learn Today

•What exposure bracketing is and when to use it

•How to set up automatic or manual bracketing on your camera

•How to shoot bracketed sequences for HDR or safety

•How to blend bracketed images (optional post-processing preview)

Key Concepts: What Is Exposure Bracketing?

Bracketing means capturing multiple versions of the same scene at different exposures.

A typical 3 shot bracketing sequence looks like this:

- •Image 1: Underexposed (captures highlight detail)

- •Image 2: Neutral (base exposure)

- •Image 3: Overexposed (captures shadow detail)

Your camera can often do this automatically using the AEB (Auto Exposure Bracketing)feature, or you can manually change your settings between shots.

Step-by-Step Exercise: Exposure Bracketing Practice

Today, you'll bracket a challenging scene using both manual and automatic methods. You'll then compare the results and observe how detail is preserved.

What You Need

- •DSLR or mirrorless camera with bracketing capability (AEB)

- •Tripod (strongly recommended for precise alignment)

- •Scene with bright highlights and dark shadows (e.g., sunlit window, outdoor scene with sky and shade)

- •Manual or Aperture Priority mode

Step 1: Find a High-Contrast Scene

Choose a composition with:

- A bright sky or window

- Deep shadows or dark foreground

- Enough visual interest to justify preserving both ends of the tonal range

Step 2: Enable Auto Exposure Bracketing (AEB)

Check your camera manual if needed, but usually:

- In the menu, look for "Exposure Bracketing" or "AEB"

- Set it to 3 shots at +/- 1 or 2 EV

- Use continuous shooting mode or press the shutter 3 times in a row

- Use Aperture Priority mode (Av) so only shutter speed changes between exposures

Take the bracketed set—your camera will fire three images at different exposure levels.

Step 3: Try Manual Bracketing

If your camera doesn't offer AEB, you can do it manually.

- Set the base exposure

- Take the first photo

- Adjust exposure compensation to -2 EV, shoot again

- Then adjust to +2 EV, and shoot once more

You'll end up with three photos, each emphasizing a different part of the tonal range.

Step 4: Review and Compare

Look at the three images:

- The underexposed photo: Rich in sky or highlight detail

- The normal photo: Balanced but may lose detail in highlights or shadows

- The overexposed photo: Brings out shadow details, but may blow out bright areas

Ask: yourself:

- Which image captures the most important detail?
- Could you blend these later to get the best of all three?

Step 5: Optional – Combine the Images

If you have photo editing software like Lightroom, Photoshop, or any HDR blending tool:

- Import the three bracketed shots
- Use the HDR merge or Exposure Merge feature
- Adjust highlights, shadows, and contrast to create a unified image

📌 Tip: Even if you don't merge them, just having multiple exposures gives you options when editing.

When to Use Bracketing

- Landscapes: Preserve sky and foreground detail
- Architectural Interiors: Balance window light and room shadows
- Backlit Subjects: Recover shadow detail without blowing out the light
- High-Stakes Shots: Bracket just in case, especially in tricky lighting

Why This Will Make Your Photos Better

Bracketing isn't just a safety net—it's a creative technique. It shows you the full range of light in a scene and helps you protect important details that might otherwise be lost. With practice, it becomes second nature—and can save you from disappointment later.

Even if you only use one of the images, you've given yourself more choices and a better shot at a perfect exposure.

Quick Daily Practice

- •Find a tricky lighting situation (sun through trees, a person indoors near a window, or late afternoon shadows)

- •Take a bracketed set of three images: -2, 0, +2

- •Compare how different parts of the scene are emphasized in each shot

- •Ask: Which one tells the story best?

A 5 shot exposure bracketing sequence using aperture priority

with exposure value changing 3 stops with each shot.

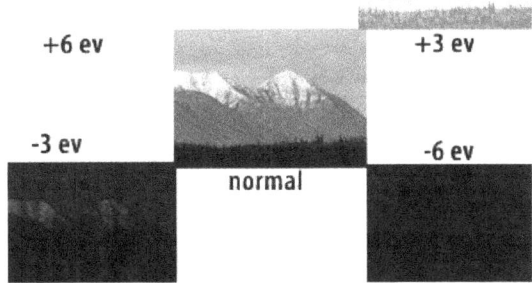

+6 ev

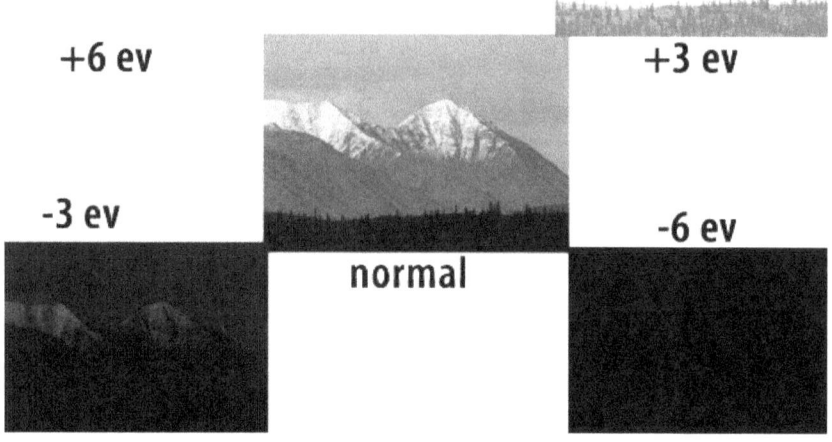

+3 ev

-3 ev

normal

-6 ev

Final Thought

Light isn't always easy to tame—but with bracketing, you don't have to choose between shadow and highlight. You can have both. The scene contains all the beauty; bracketing is how you make sure your camera captures it

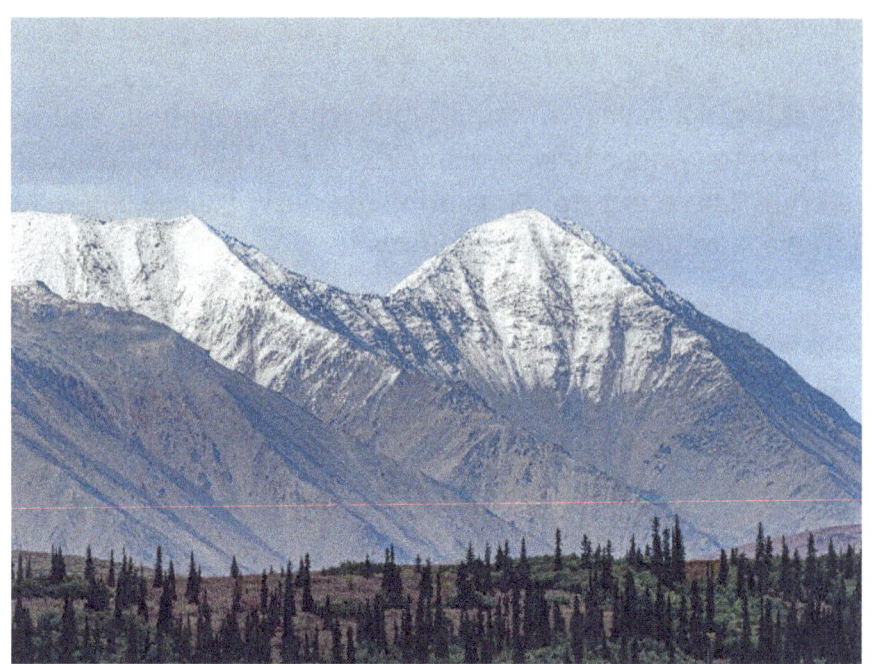

Merged HDR Image

Day 13 Reflective Journal Pages

Use these prompts to reflect after each lesson or at the end of each week. There's no right or wrong way to answer—let your thoughts flow honestly and creatively.

Day 13: Exposure Bracketing

1. What did I observe about the light today?

2. What surprised or challenged me during this lesson?

3. Which image felt the strongest—and why?

4. What would I do differently if I repeated this exercise?

5. Notes, thoughts, or ideas sparked today:

[Space for writing or sketching]

Day 14: Metering Modes

> "Your camera sees the world through light—but how it measures that light is up to you."

Why This Matters

Your camera is designed to calculate exposure automatically, but how it makes that calculation depends on the metering mode you choose. Metering is how the camera "reads" the brightness of a scene and determines what settings will produce a properly exposed image.

By default, most cameras are set to average the light across the entire frame—but that might not work if your subject is backlit, standing in shadow, or only occupies a small part of the frame. Knowing which metering mode to use—and when—gives you more control and helps you avoid common exposure mistakes.

Today's exercise introduces you to the main metering modes and how they affect your photos.

What You'll Learn Today

•What metering is and why it matters for exposure

•The three primary metering modes: Evaluative, Center-Weighted, and Spot

•When to use each mode for better results

•How metering affects images with tricky lighting (e.g., backlit subjects)

Key Concepts: Understanding Metering Modes

Most DSLR and mirrorless cameras offer these three metering options:

1. Evaluative (Matrix) Metering

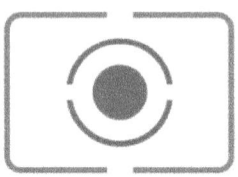

- •Measures light across the entire frame

- •Weighs exposure based on focus point and scene brightness

- •Default mode on most cameras

- •Great for balanced lighting or general use

Evaluative metering

2. Center-Weighted Metering

- •Measures the entire frame but prioritizes the center

- •Ignores edges of the frame

- •Good for portraits or off-center lighting when the subject is in the middle

Centre weighted average

3. Spot Metering

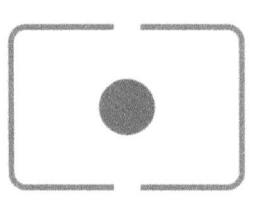

- •Measures only a small area (often 1–5% of the frame)

- •Usually linked to your focus point

- •Best for backlit scenes, high-contrast subjects, or bright highlights

Spot metering

- •

Step-by-Step Exercise: Comparing Metering Modes

You'll photograph the same subject in the same lighting using each metering mode and compare the results.

What You Need

- •DSLR or mirrorless camera with selectable metering modes

- •Scene with uneven lighting (e.g., subject by a window, backlit object, or patchy shade)

- •Manual or Aperture Priority mode

- •A tripod (optional)

Step 1: Set to Evaluative Metering

- •Choose a high-contrast scene (e.g., a person in shadow next to a bright window).

- •Set your camera to Evaluative (Matrix) Metering (check your manual or menu).

- •Set Aperture Priority and a medium aperture (f/5.6 or f/8).

- •Focus on the subject and take a photo.

Note: Evaluative tries to balance everything. If the background is much brighter than the subject, your subject might be underexposed.

Step 2: Switch to Center-Weighted Metering

- •Keep the composition the same.

- •Switch metering to Center-Weighted.

- •Focus again and take the photo.

Note: If your subject is centered, you'll likely see better exposure on them —but the background might lose detail.

Step 3: Try Spot Metering

•Switch metering to Spot.

•Ensure your focus point is on the brightest or most important part of the subject (e.g., face or eye).

•Take the photo.

Note: The subject will be correctly exposed but the rest of the frame may go very dark or very bright depending on overall light contrast.

Step 4: Review and Compare

Compare the three images side by side:

•Which version exposes your subject best?

•Which version balances the scene as a whole?

•Did one version preserve important highlights or shadows better?

Make notes about how the metering modes shifted exposure priorities—and which would have worked best for your creative goal.

When to Use Each Metering Mode

Mode	Best For
Evaluative	General scenes with even light
Center-Weighted	Portraits with consistent central subject
Spot	High contrast scenes, backlight, tricky light

Why This Will Make Your Photos Better

Metering is how your camera makes decisions about exposure. When you learn to override or guide those decisions, your exposures become more consistent—and more creative.

No more blown-out skies or underexposed faces. No more "guess and check." Just clear, intentional control over how your camera interprets the light.

Quick Daily Practice

•Choose a tricky lighting scene and photograph it using all three metering modes.

•Focus on the same spot each time and compare how the exposure shifts.

•Ask: Which one best matched your vision for the image?

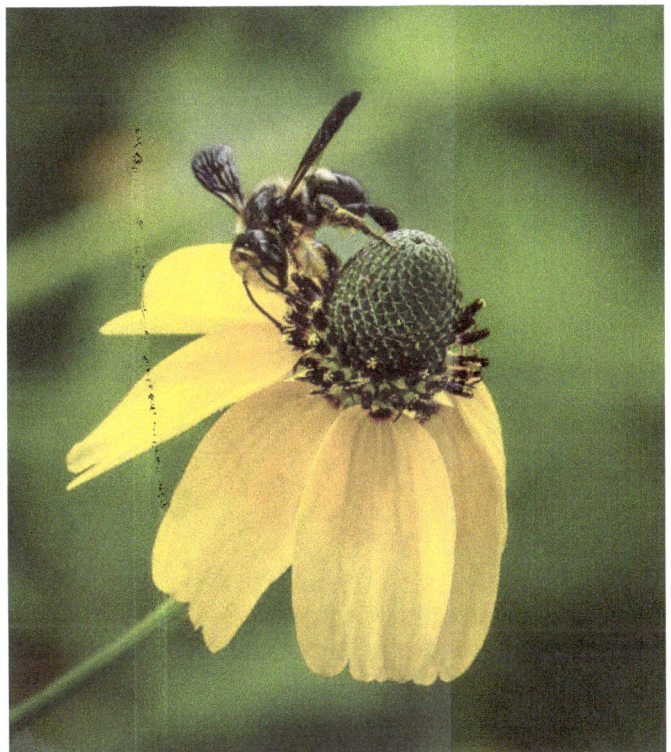

Center-weighted Average Metering

Final Thought

Your camera doesn't know what's important in the frame—you do. Metering modes let you tell the camera where to pay attention. Master this, and you move from reactive to deliberate. That's when your photography truly starts to reflect yourvision.

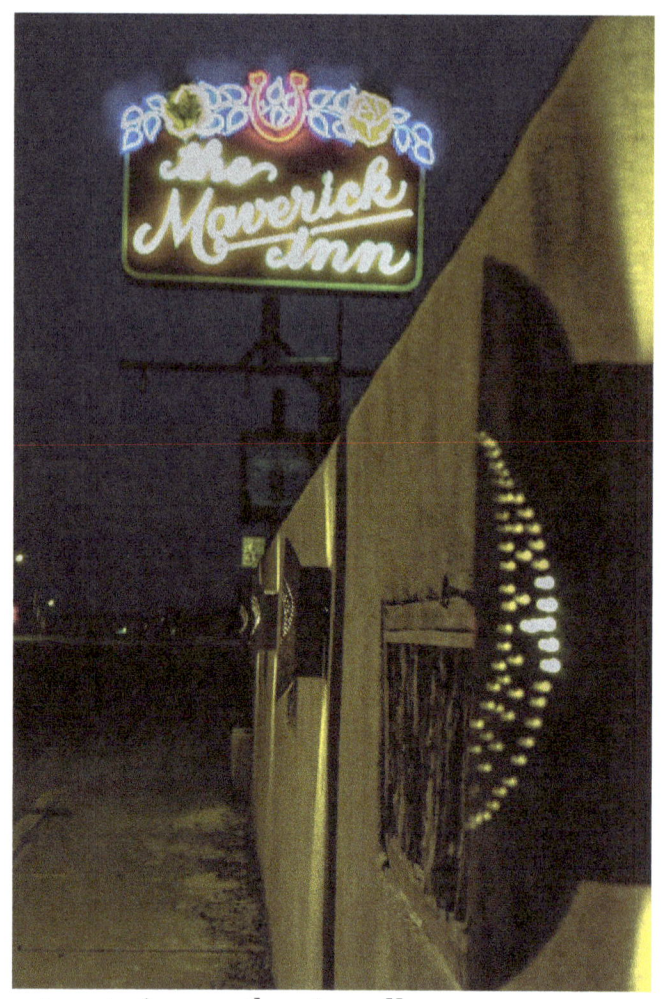

A scene where spot metering on the sign allow me go capture it fully lit.

Day 14 Reflective Journal Pages

Use these prompts to reflect after each lesson or at the end of each week. There's no right or wrong way to answer—let your thoughts flow honestly and creatively.

Day 14: Metering Modes

1. What did I observe about the light today?

2. What surprised or challenged me during this lesson?

3. Which image felt the strongest—and why?

4. What would I do differently if I repeated this exercise?

5. Notes, thoughts, or ideas sparked today:

[Space for writing or sketching]

Week 2 Reflection: Exposure & Camera Settings

If Week 1 taught you to see the light, Week 2 taught you to control it.

This week you stepped into the technical heart of photography—learning how to balance aperture, shutter speed, and ISO to expose an image just the way you envision it. You practiced freezing motion, controlling depth of field, working in low light, and reading a histogram with confidence.

These lessons may have stretched you—and that's a good thing. Mastery doesn't happen overnight, but with every image, you've strengthened your understanding of how your camera sees the world. Most importantly, you've started making intentional decisions instead of relying on auto mode. That's the moment when photography becomes art.

Keep going—you're building control, creative freedom, and trust in your own eye.

In Week 2, you gained control over the technical heart of photography: exposure. Through hands-on exercises and real-world scenarios, you explored how to balance the three core camera settings— aperture, shutter speed, and ISO—to shape both the brightness and the creative feel of your images.

Congratulate yourself! You've learned to:

- •Use aperture to create dreamy blur or sharp depth
- •Control motion with fast or slow shutter speeds
- •Adapt to dark scenes by adjusting ISO without fear
- •Read your histogram like a truth-teller, not a guess

•Capture full dynamic range with exposure bracketing

•Guide your camera's attention through different metering modes

By the end of the week, you weren't just reacting to the camera—you were making conscious, creative decisions about how your images looked and felt. You now understand how light enters the camera and how to shape exposure to serve your vision.

Week 3 Introduction: Composition with Light

Light is only part of the equation—composition is the other half of storytelling. Now that you know how to control exposure, it's time to focus on how light shapes what we see, where we look, and how we feel in an image.

In Week 3, you'll explore how to:

- Use light to create powerful silhouettes

- Sculpt scenes with shadow for emotion and depth

- Capture soft, natural window light in portraits

- Highlight your subject using reflected or bounced light

- Arrange light and elements using proven compositional techniques

You'll begin to think more like a visual designer—placing light and shadow with intention and crafting scenes that draw the viewer in.

This week is about artistry. You already know how to expose the light—now, you'll learn how to compose with it.

Day 15: Silhouettes

"Sometimes, the strongest story is told in shadow."

Why This Matters

A silhouette is a visual whisper that speaks volumes. By reducing your subject to shape and outline, silhouettes remove detail—but amplify emotion. They rely on bold contrast and strong composition, making them one of the most compelling ways to use light artistically.

Creating a silhouette requires you to expose for the bright background, leaving your subject in shadow. It's a creative choice that simplifies the frame and invites the viewer's imagination to fill in the blanks.

Mastering silhouettes sharpens your eye for shape, line, and light direction—all essential compositional tools.

What You'll Learn Today

- •How to photograph strong, intentional silhouettes

- •What kinds of light and subjects work best

- •How to expose for the background to create deep shadows

- •How to compose with shape and negative space

Key Concepts: What Is a Silhouette?

A silhouette occurs when your subject is completely backlit and rendered as a dark shape against a bright background.

- •The subject is underexposed, showing no internal detail

- •The background is bright, usually from the sky, window, or sun

•The subject's shape and outline must be instantly recognizable

📌 You're telling a story with form, not detail.

Step-by-Step Exercise: Create a Bold Silhouette

You'll create several silhouette images, both natural and posed, by exposing for the background.

What You Need

- •DSLR or mirrorless camera

- •A subject with a clear, simple shape (person, tree, object, animal)

- •A bright background (sunset, sky, window, or doorway)

- •Aperture Priority or Manual mode

Step 1: Find the Right Light and Angle

The key to a silhouette is backlighting—the light must be coming from behind your subject and facing your camera.

📌 Good options include:

- •Sunrise or sunset

- •Open sky behind a person or tree

- •Indoors with a subject in front of a bright window

Step 2: Compose the Scene with Shape in Mind

Choose a subject that has a recognizable outline. For people:

- •Profile views work best (showing nose, chin, limbs)

- •Avoid overlapping limbs or objects behind them

📌 Keep the background clean and uncluttered. Silhouettes thrive on simplicity.

Step 3: Expose for the Background

Set your camera to Aperture Priority (A or Av) or Manual mode.

- •Point your camera at the brightest part of the background

- •Use exposure lock (AE-L) or exposure compensation (-1 to -2 stops)

- •Focus on your subject's edge or manually set focus

Take the shot. Your subject should be dark or black, and the background correctly exposed.

Step 4: Adjust and Refine

Take multiple shots:

- •Move your subject or yourself to improve the outline

- •Try placing the subject off-center for a more dynamic composition

- •Look for frames within frames (e.g., silhouetted figure in a doorway)

Experiment with different apertures (f/4 to f/8) to control sharpness and background clarity.

Step 5: Review and Analyze

Compare your silhouette photos and ask:

- •Is the subject's shape clear and readable?

- •Does the composition feel balanced and intentional?

- •Did you lose any important details by underexposing?

Note what worked and what could be simplified next time.

When to Use Silhouettes

•To convey emotion through posture, gesture, or outline

•To simplify a scene and remove distractions

•To create drama or mystery

•When you want the light and shape to speak louder than the detail

Why This Will Make Your Photos Better

Silhouettes push you to see differently. You're not relying on expression, color, or texture—you're composing with form and light alone. This strengthens your understanding of visual storytelling and trains you to recognize strong subjects and graphic shapes.

Plus, silhouettes are often powerful, poetic, and timeless.

Quick Daily Practice

•Go outside near sunset or face a bright window indoors.

•Choose a subject and try at least 3 different compositions.

•Make sure the background is exposed properly and the subject's shape is readable.

•Post your favorite and ask yourself: What's the story this shape tells?

Final Thought

Silhouettes remind us that less can be more. That mystery can speak louder than detail. That sometimes, the strongest light is behind us—and the most powerful moment is defined by shadow.

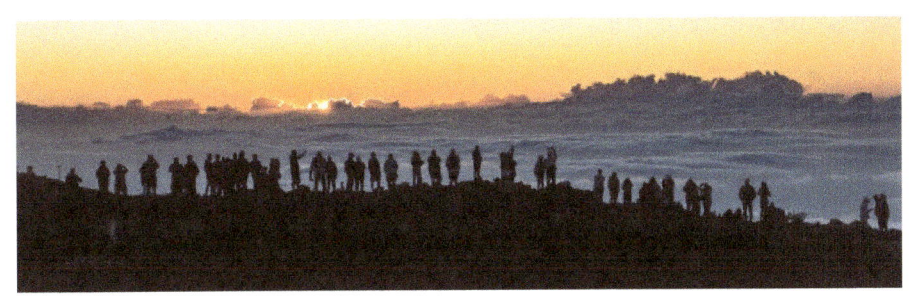

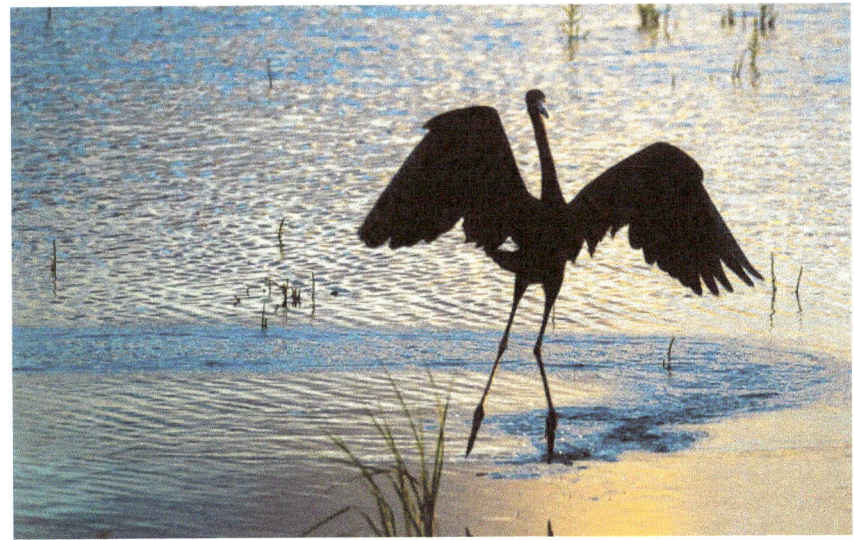

145

Day 15 Reflective Journal Pages

Use these prompts to reflect after each lesson or at the end of each week. There's no right or wrong way to answer—let your thoughts flow honestly and creatively.

Day 15: Silhouettes

1. What did I observe about the light today?

2. What surprised or challenged me during this lesson?

3. Which image felt the strongest—and why?

4. What would I do differently if I repeated this exercise?

5. Notes, thoughts, or ideas sparked today:

[Space for writing or sketching]

Day 16: Shadows as Shape

> "Light reveals—but shadows define."

Why This Matters

We often chase the perfect light, but forget the equal power of its partner: shadow. Shadows add depth, form, and mystery. They carve dimension into a scene and guide the eye by contrast. And sometimes, the shadow itself becomes the subject—a bold, graphic shape that tells a story all its own.

Learning to see shadows as compositional elements changes how you photograph. You'll stop seeing them as distractions to avoid—and start recognizing them as tools for strong visual design, emotional impact, and even storytelling.

What You'll Learn Today

- How to use shadows as shapes in your compositions
- How light angle and intensity affect shadow form
- How to position yourself and your subject to emphasize shadows
- How to photograph both cast shadows and form shadows

Key Concepts: What Are Shadows in Photography?

There are two types of shadows to look for:

- Cast Shadows: Created when your subject blocks light, leaving a shape on a surface (e.g., a person's shadow on the ground).

- Form Shadows: The shaded side of the subject itself (e.g., one side of a face in side light).

In both cases, shadows add shape, contrast, and structure—and can become key compositional elements.

Step-by-Step Exercise: Shadow Play

Today, you'll photograph a subject and its shadow together, emphasizing the relationship between light and dark.

What You Need

- DSLR or mirrorless camera

- A strong directional light source (sunlight, window light, flashlight)

- A subject with clear edges (person, plant, object, or architecture)

- A blank surface like pavement, wall, or tabletop to catch cast shadows

Step 1: Choose Strong Directional Light

Look for:

- Morning or late afternoon sun for long, defined shadows

- Window light for side shadows on a face or object

- Artificial light (like a lamp or flashlight) if shooting indoors

📌 The lower the light angle, the longer and more dramatic the shadows.

Step 2: Position Your Subject Thoughtfully

Place your subject so it casts a bold shadow onto a surface.

Try:

- A hand reaching into sunlight on a wall

- A chair or flower casting a shadow across the ground

- A person standing in angled sun, casting a long shadow behind them

Photograph the shadow as part of the composition—not just the subject.

Step 3: Compose with the Shadow in Mind

Experiment with:

- Top-down views of shadows on the ground

- Shooting only the shadow (letting it represent the subject)

- Including both the subject and its shadow in creative framing

- Leading lines or symmetry created by the shadow

Take multiple compositions: full subject, partial shadow, just the shadow.

Step 4: Adjust Exposure for Drama

Try exposing for the highlight to deepen the shadow (using -1 to -2 EV compensation).

Then try exposing for the shadow to retain more detail in dark areas.

Compare how exposure changes the mood and clarity of the shadow.

Step 5: Review and Reflect

Ask:

- Which image uses the shadow as a subject, not just a side effect?

- How does the shape of the shadow change the composition?

- Did the shadow add mood, mystery, or motion?

Make note of the lighting angle and how it affected your results.

When to Use Shadows Creatively

- •To add contrast and depth to flat scenes

- •To emphasize gesture or movement

- •To create graphic or abstract compositions

- •To suggest emotion: mystery, drama, nostalgia, or solitude

Why This Will Make Your Photos Better

Shadows teach you to think three-dimensionally. They help your photos move beyond the literal and into the expressive. When you compose with shadows, you start using negative space, suggestion, and visual rhythm to lead the viewer's eye—and evoke a feeling.

This is when your photography becomes not just skillful, but artful.

Quick Daily Practice

- •Walk around your home or neighborhood during golden hour.
- •Look for cast shadows on walls, sidewalks, and tabletops.
- •Photograph a scene with the subject and again just the shadow.
- •Ask: What does the shadow say that the subject doesn't?

Final Thought

A shadow is not an absence of light—it's a shape sculpted by it. When you begin to see shadows as design elements, your photography gains a new language. A quieter, subtler one—but no less powerful.

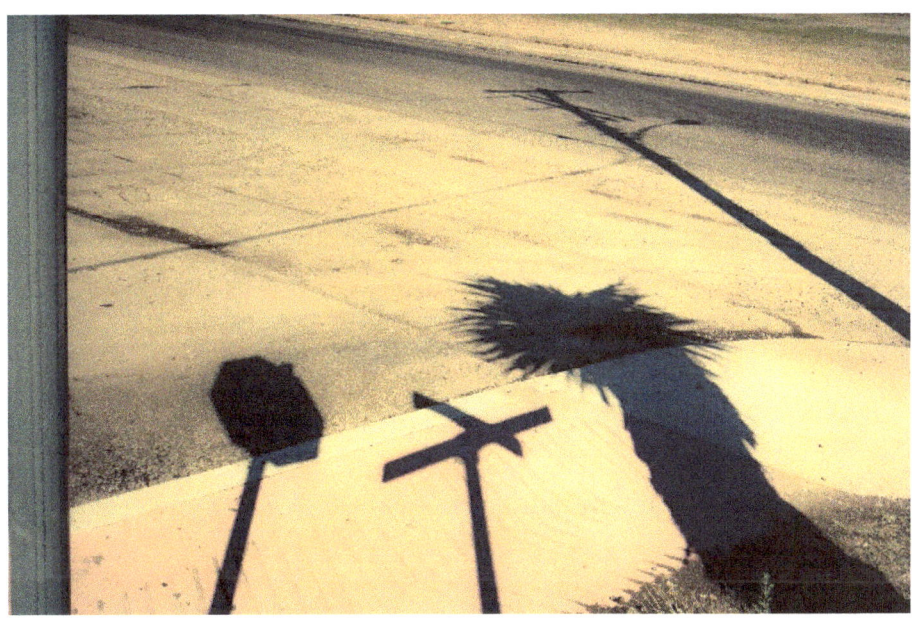

This photograph, taken on a sunlit corner in Alpine, Texas, captures the distinct shadows cast by a stop sign, a street sign, and a palm tree—transforming everyday objects into bold, graphic elements. The strong sunlight creates crisp, angular shadows that stretch across the ground, separating the shapes from their physical sources and turning them into abstract forms and compositional lines. As explored in Day 16, shadows can become just as important as the objects casting them—adding visual interest, rhythm, and balance to an image. In this photo, the scene feels less about signage or landscape, and more about the geometry of light and shape, emphasizing how shadows can serve as both subject and design.

Day 16 Reflective Journal Pages

Use these prompts to reflect after each lesson or at the end of each week. There's no right or wrong way to answer—let your thoughts flow honestly and creatively.

Day 16: Shadows as Shape

1. What did I observe about the light today?

2. What surprised or challenged me during this lesson?

3. Which image felt the strongest—and why?

4. What would I do differently if I repeated this exercise?

5. Notes, thoughts, or ideas sparked today:

[Space for writing or sketching]

Day 17: Window Light Portraits

"A window is more than a source of light—it's a natural portrait studio."

Why This Matters

You don't need expensive lighting gear to create stunning, professional-looking portraits. All you need is a window and the ability to observe how light behaves.

Window light is soft, directional, and easy to control. It's ideal for portraits because it flatters the subject, reveals texture gently, and creates depth with subtle shadows. Whether you're photographing a person or a still life, learning how to work with window light will elevate your work —fast.

Understanding how to position your subject in relation to a window will help you create a variety of looks, from bright and airy to dramatic and moody. You'll also strengthen your awareness of direction, quality, and falloff—essential skills for any photographer.

What You'll Learn Today

- •How to position your subject in relation to a window for different effects
- •The difference between front, side, and back window light
- •How to use reflectors or whiteboards to balance shadows
- •How to meter and expose for natural indoor light

Key Concepts: Why Window Light Works

Window light is typically:

153

- Soft (especially with curtains or overcast days)
- Directional (giving shape and depth)
- Constant (you can see exactly what you're working with)

It's a perfect tool for beginners and a beloved technique of professionals.

Step-by-Step Exercise: Natural Light Portrait at a Window

Today, you'll create a portrait or still life using window light in three ways: side light, front light, and backlight.

What You Need

- DSLR or mirrorless camera
- A person willing to pose (or a still life subject)
- A window with indirect light (curtains optional)
- Optional: white foam board or reflector, chair or table, tripod

Step 1: Side Light Setup

Position your subject next to the window, with the window to their left or right.

- Sit or place the subject about 1–2 feet from the window
- The window should be the only light source if possible
- Use a white reflector or foam board on the opposite side to bounce light into shadows if needed

Focus on the eye closest to the light. Shoot at f/2.8–f/5.6 to soften background.

This setup creates natural Rembrandt-style light, with gentle shadows and dimension.

Step 2: Front Light Setup

Now have your subject face the window directly, with you between them and the window.

- This creates flat, even lighting—no strong shadows

- Works well for soft portraits and glowing skin tones
- Move the subject closer to the window for brighter light or back for softer falloff

Ideal for bright, friendly portraits or soft still life images.

Step 3: Backlight Setup

Turn the subject so the window is behind them, and you are facing into the light.

- You may need to increase exposure compensation (+1 or +2 EV) to avoid underexposing the subject
- Optional: Place a reflector in front of the subject to bounce light back onto their face
- This setup creates a glow or halo effect, especially on hair or translucent objects

This technique is moodier and more artistic—be prepared to experiment.

Step 4: Review and Reflect

Look at all three images side-by-side.

Ask:

- How does the direction of light change the mood?
- Which photo shows the most depth or flattering shadows?
- Did the reflector improve the light balance?

Note how small shifts in position made a big difference in the outcome.

Tips for Window Light Portraits

- •Sheer curtains make great diffusers for harsh window light

- •North-facing windows provide consistent soft light throughout the day

- •Avoid direct sun on faces unless you want dramatic contrast

- •Always focus on the eye—that's the emotional anchor of a portrait

- •Use a reflector (or even a white pillowcase or foam board) to fill in shadows

Why This Will Make Your Photos Better

Window light is one of the most accessible, controllable, and beautiful sources of natural light. It teaches you how to see direction, falloff, and catchlights without overwhelming you with gear.

With nothing but a window and a bit of awareness, you'll start creating portraits that feel timeless, intentional, and emotionally connected.

Quick Daily Practice

•Choose a window in your home and photograph the same subject with:

  •Side light

  •Front light

  •Back light

•Use a reflector on one version, and skip it on another

•Observe how skin tones, shadows, and background blur change

Final Thought

You don't need a studio to make beautiful portraits—you just need a window and the courage to see the light. Whether soft and glowing or bold and dramatic, window light gives you a simple, powerful way to practice photography as both craft and art.

This portrait of a baby, lit by natural window light from his right side, is a classic example of how soft, directional light can bring warmth, intimacy, and dimension to a photograph. The window acts as a large, diffused light source—wrapping gently around his face, creating a natural gradient of highlights and shadows. The result is a portrait that feels both honest and timeless, where the light not only illuminates his features but also conveys mood and presence. As explored in Day 17, window light offers a beautifully controlled environment for portraiture, allowing texture, expression, and emotion to come through without harshness. This image reminds us that sometimes the most powerful lighting setups are the simplest—and often right at home.

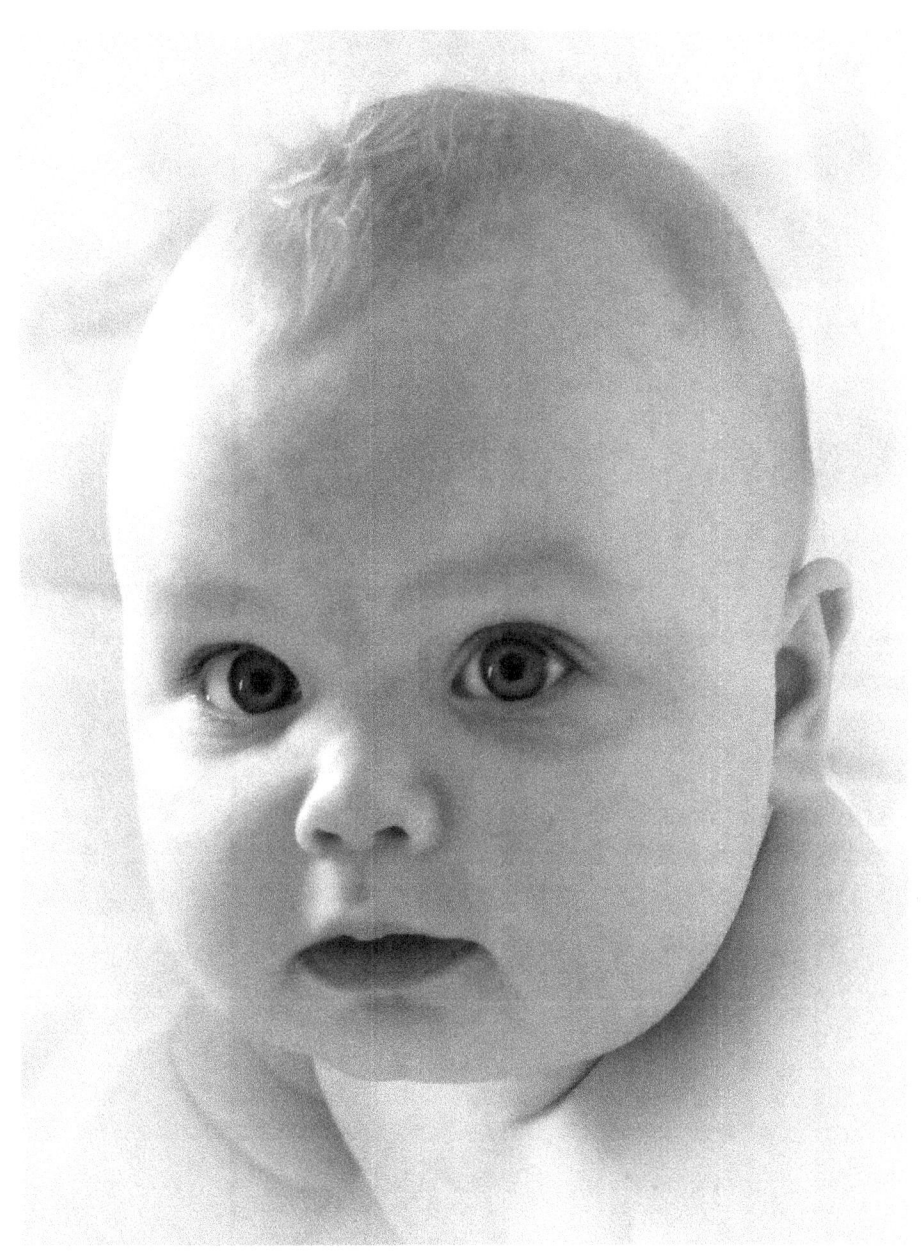

Day 17 Reflective Journal Pages

Use these prompts to reflect after each lesson or at the end of each week. There's no right or wrong way to answer—let your thoughts flow honestly and creatively.

Day 17: Window Light Portraits

1. What did I observe about the light today?

2. What surprised or challenged me during this lesson?

3. Which image felt the strongest—and why?

4. What would I do differently if I repeated this exercise?

5. Notes, thoughts, or ideas sparked today:

[Space for writing or sketching]

Day 18: Using Reflected and Bounced Light

"Light doesn't have to come straight from the source—
sometimes its second stop is where the magic happens."

Why This Matters

Not all beautiful light is direct. Some of the most flattering, subtle, and balanced illumination comes from reflected or bounced light—when light hits a surface and spreads softly onto your subject.

Think about the gentle glow from a white wall, the warm tones of light bouncing off sand or grass, or the even lighting you get when using a reflector. Reflected light reduces harsh shadows, evens out skin tones, and reveals detail in places that direct light can't reach—without adding extra gear or cost.

Learning how to see and use bounced light trains you to become a sculptor of light, not just a seeker of it.

What You'll Learn Today

- •The difference between reflected and bounced light
- •How to find and use natural reflectors (walls, floors, ceilings)
- •How to position white cards, reflectors, or foam boards
- •How to use reflected light to improve portraits and still life images

•

Key Concepts: What Is Reflected and Bounced Light?

Reflected light happens when light bounces off a surface and spreads into shadowed areas.

Common reflectors include:
- •White walls or ceilings (neutral, soft light)
- •Sidewalks or light-colored ground (cool, upward fill)
- •Beige, golden, or sandy surfaces (warm fill)
- •Green grass (can add unwanted color cast—use with care)

Bounced light is often intentionally directed using tools like:
- •White foam boards or cards
- •Silver/gold reflectors
- •Portable 5-in-1 reflector kits
- •Even white clothing or paper in a pinch

Step-by-Step Exercise: Enhancing a Portrait with Bounce Light

You'll photograph the same subject with and without bounced light to observe how it changes shadow and mood.

What You Need
- •DSLR or mirrorless camera
- •A subject (person or object) placed near a window or under soft directional light
- •A white foam board, poster board, or reflector (even a white towel will work)
- •Aperture Priority or Manual mode

Step 1: Find Side Light and a Shadowed Subject

Place your subject next to a window so light hits them from one side, leaving the opposite side in shadow.

> •This setup exaggerates contrast and gives you a clear before-and-after comparison.

> •Set your camera to f/2.8–f/5.6 for a softly focused background.

Take a photo without any reflector to capture the natural lighting.

Step 2: Add a Reflector

Now hold or position the white board or reflector on the shadow side of the subject.

> •Angle it to catch the incoming window light and bounce it back onto the face or object.

> •You'll see the shadow soften and the light fill in more evenly.

> •You may even catch a subtle catchlight in the eyes.

Take another photo with the reflector in place.

Optional: Try reflectors with different surfaces (white, silver, gold) and compare how each one affects the warmth and intensity of the bounced light.

Step 3: Move the Reflector for Control

Try:

> •Closer = more fill

> •Farther = softer fill

> •Angle up from below for under-chin shadows

> •Angle down from above for soft overhead fill

Take a few variations and note how each change affects the subject's look and mood.

Step 4: Observe Ambient Reflectors in the Environment

Step outside and look around:

> •Are there walls, concrete sidewalks, light-colored fences, or open umbrellas nearby?

> •Do they bounce light back onto faces, flowers, or architecture?

Take a photo of a subject with and without the natural reflected light and compare.

Review and Reflect

Ask:

> •Which version looks more polished or professional?
> •Did the reflector help bring out detail or eye catchlights?
> •Which bounce surface gave the best tone and softness?

Record which tools or locations you'd use again for future shoots.

Tips for Using Reflected and Bounced Light

> •White bounce = neutral fill (softest and most natural)

> •Silver bounce = bright, crisp light (adds punch but can be intense)

> •Gold bounce = warm tones (great for skin in warm light)

> •Green grass or colored walls = may cast unwanted tints—watch your color balance

> •Angle is everything—tilt the surface until you see the bounce

Why This Will Make Your Photos Better

Reflectors and bounced light give you lighting control—without a studio. You can soften shadows, improve portraits, and shoot confidently in mixed lighting just by redirecting what's already there.

Learning to see light bouncing around a scene transforms how you photograph. Suddenly, you'll notice opportunities for soft fill light in places you used to pass by. Your images will feel more intentional, balanced, and professionally lit—even with simple tools.

Quick Daily Practice

- Photograph a subject next to a window or lamp.
- Take one photo without and one with a reflector.
- Try bouncing light from different sides and distances.
- Observe how the light shapes your subject, not just illuminates it.

Final Thought

Photographers don't just chase light—they redirect it. Using reflected and bounced light lets you shape the scene, bring softness to contrast, and create harmony between subject and shadow. Once you learn to bend the light to your will, there's no going back.

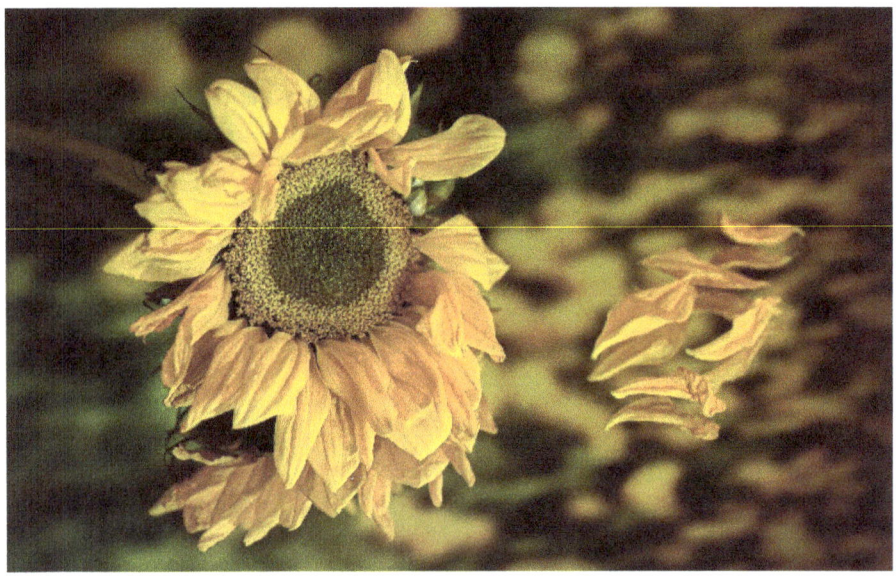

This photograph of a sunflower was created in a controlled studio setup, using a right-side key light, a mirror, and a gold reflector—a perfect example of how reflected and bounced light can shape mood and highlight detail. The main light casts gentle directional illumination, while the gold reflector bounces warm, glowing light back into the center of the flower, enhancing the richness of its tones and drawing attention to the intricate textures of the seeds. A strategically placed mirror adds a reflection and a subtle fill to the shadowed areas at the bottom of the flower, softening contrast without flattening the scene. As taught in Day 18, reflected light allows you to control exposure, create depth, and add character to your subject—all without introducing a second direct light source. This image shows how thoughtful light placement and reflection can elevate a studio photo from simple to sculptural.

Day 18 Reflective Journal Pages

Use these prompts to reflect after each lesson or at the end of each week. There's no right or wrong way to answer—let your thoughts flow honestly and creatively.

Day 18: Using Reflected and Bounced Light

1. What did I observe about the light today?

2. What surprised or challenged me during this lesson?

3. Which image felt the strongest—and why?

4. What would I do differently if I repeated this exercise?

5. Notes, thoughts, or ideas sparked today:

[Space for writing or sketching]

Day 19: Leading the Eye with Light

"Where the light falls, the eye follows."

Why This Matters

Light isn't just about visibility—it's about direction. As photographers, we're not only capturing what's in front of the lens; we're guiding the viewer's journey through the frame. And one of the most powerful ways to do that is by using light as a visual pathway.

By highlighting some areas and letting others fall into shadow, you can direct attention to what matters most in your image. This concept is known as visual hierarchy—and light is one of the fastest ways to establish it.

When you learn to lead the eye with light, your compositions become more intentional, more compelling, and more likely to hold a viewer's attention.

What You'll Learn Today

- How light naturally guides the viewer's attention
- How to use contrast, brightness, and shadow to emphasize your subject
- Where to place your subject relative to the brightest part of the frame
- How to use light to support composition and storytelling

Key Concepts: How Light Leads the Eye

The human eye is drawn to:

- Bright areas before dark ones

- High contrast areas over flat tones

- Sharp focus areas over soft or blurry ones

- Warm light over cool light

📌 This means you can manipulate exposure and composition to control what the viewer sees first—and what they remember.

Step-by-Step Exercise: Composing with Light Hierarchy

Today, you'll photograph a subject using light placement and exposure to guide the viewer's eye through the frame.

What You Need

- DSLR or mirrorless camera

- A scene with directional light (e.g., window, shaft of sunlight, lamp)

- A subject with shape or detail (person, object, texture)

- Optional: reflector or black card for shadow control

- Aperture Priority or Manual mode

Step 1: Place the Light Where You Want Attention

Set up your subject so that the most important part (e.g., a face, flower, detail) is lit more brightly than the rest of the scene.

Try:

- Positioning your subject in a spotlight or shaft of window light

- Using side light to create a gradient from light to dark across the frame

- Letting the background or edges fall into soft shadow

Compose so the eye naturally moves toward the light and pauses on your subject.

Step 2: Use Negative Space or Shadow to Control the Frame

Let non-essential areas fall into darkness or blur by:

- •Positioning those areas farther from the light

- •Using a narrow aperture to isolate your subject

- •Lowering your exposure slightly (try -1 EV compensation) for a more dramatic effect

Take a few variations with more or less background detail.

Step 3: Lead the Eye Through Light Transitions

Create compositions where light moves across the frame, guiding the viewer.

Try:

- •A path of dappled light on a sidewalk or through leaves
- •A highlight on a subject leading to a brighter background
- •A hand or gesture reaching into the light

Take at least one photo where the eye travels through 2–3 levels of brightness.

Step 4: Review and Reflect

Compare your images and ask:

- •Where does your eye go first?

- •Did light lead you to the subject—or away from it?

- •Could you simplify the composition further by hiding or darkening distractions?

Make note of one change you'd make next time to improve clarity or impact.

Tips for Leading the Eye with Light

- •Brightness = attention magnet

- •Keep your subject the brightest or most contrasty area in the frame

- Avoid distractions like bright objects or blown-out areas near the edges
- Use vignetting or darkened corners to hold focus inward
- Let shadows play a supportive role—not everything needs to be seen

Why This Will Make Your Photos Better

Learning to guide the eye with light helps your images become clearer, stronger, and more engaging. It's one of the marks of a skilled photographer: the ability to control not just the light, but the story the light tells.

Your compositions will stop feeling accidental—and start feeling designed.

Quick Daily Practice

- Find a scene with mixed light (window, late afternoon sun, or shaded light pool)
- Place an object or subject in the brightest area
- Take 2–3 shots, each with a different light emphasis
- Observe which one draws the eye most effectively

Final Thought

Light is your invisible guide, gently pulling the viewer where you want them to go. When you learn to compose not just with light, but through light, you become more than a photographer—you become a storyteller.

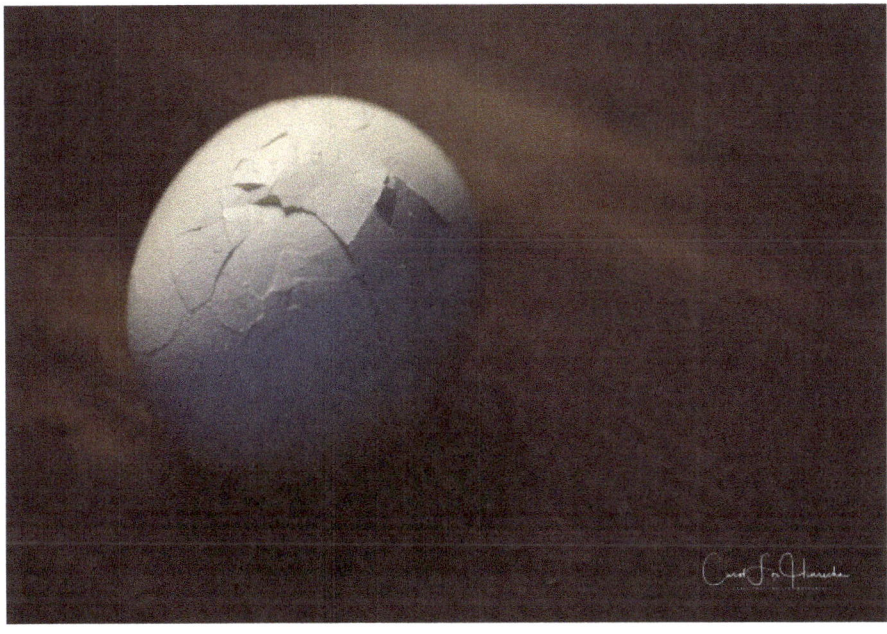

This photograph of a cracked, boiled egg uses intentional lighting to guide the viewer's attention directly to the point of impact. By concentrating the light source on the fractured shell and allowing the surrounding area to fall into shadow, I created a natural focal point. The eye is immediately drawn to the intricate lines and texture where the break occurred—an example of how light can serve as a compositional tool to lead, not just illuminate.

As explored in Day 19, effective use of light can act like a visual spotlight, helping you tell the viewer exactly where to look. In this image, the crack isn't just a flaw—it becomes the subject, framed and emphasized entirely through the way the light falls.

Day 19 Reflective Journal Pages

Use these prompts to reflect after each lesson or at the end of each week. There's no right or wrong way to answer—let your thoughts flow honestly and creatively.

Day 19: Leading the Eye with Light

1. What did I observe about the light today?

2. What surprised or challenged me during this lesson?

3. Which image felt the strongest—and why?

4. What would I do differently if I repeated this exercise?

5. Notes, thoughts, or ideas sparked today:

[Space for writing or sketching]

Day 20: Light and the Rule of Thirds

"When light meets structure, visual harmony is born."

Why This Matters

The Rule of Thirds is one of the most well-known—and widely used—compositional tools in photography. It helps create balance, movement, and interest by placing your subject off-center, along imaginary gridlines that divide your frame into thirds.

But when you combine this principle with thoughtful use of light, you elevate your compositions from well-arranged to emotionally compelling. Light doesn't just fall randomly—it can be placed, just like a subject. When you align both light and subject along the Rule of Thirds, your image gains rhythm, tension, and flow.

Today's exercise helps you pair deliberate framing with deliberate lighting to create strong, storytelling compositions.

What You'll Learn Today

•How to apply the Rule of Thirds to light placement—not just subject

•How to use bright areas or light transitions as compositional anchors

•How off-center lighting adds interest and movement

•How to refine your framing based on how light enters the frame

Key Concepts: The Rule of Thirds in Photography

Imagine dividing your frame into a 3×3 grid—two horizontal lines and two vertical lines.

- •The four intersections are key "power points"

- •Placing your subject or key light at or near one of these points increases visual impact

- •This creates asymmetry, which feels more dynamic and natural than centering everything

💡 The Rule of Thirds isn't a rule—it's a guide. But it works because it mimics how we naturally scan an image.

Step-by-Step Exercise: Composing with Light in Thirds

Today, you'll compose multiple images using the Rule of Thirds, deliberately placing both your subject and your light source on or near the gridlines.

What You Need

- •DSLR or mirrorless camera with grid overlay turned on (or visualize the thirds)

- •A subject (person, plant, object) with clear light falling on it

- •A directional light source (window, lamp, sun)

- •Optional: tripod or reflector

Step 1: Use the Grid to Compose

Turn on your camera's 3×3 grid overlay (usually found in display or viewfinder settings).

•Place your subject near one of the four intersections

•Align key elements (eye, hand, flower head, object edge) with the vertical or horizontal lines

•Let the brightest part of the light also fall near a line or intersection

Take one photo using the Rule of Thirds—and one where everything is centered. Compare the energy and balance of each.

Step 2: Shift the Light

Try shifting your subject or camera so:

•The light source (window, lamp glow, sun patch) falls into one-third of the frame

•The subject is either within that light—or just at the edge of it

•Shadow fills the remaining two-thirds

This technique creates tension and interest by using light placement as part of the composition.

Step 3: Use Negative Space

Leave part of the frame empty or dark to:

•Balance the brighter or more detailed side

•Let light travel across the thirds

•Create a sense of openness, solitude, or breathing room

Compose with your subject on one third and let light fade into shadow across the remaining space.

Step 4: Review and Reflect

Look at your images and ask:

•Does the Rule of Thirds guide the viewer's eye more effectively?

•How does the placement of light support or distract from the subject?

•Did the photo feel more dynamic or more balanced when light and subject aligned with the grid?

Make a note about which image felt most harmonious—and which broke the rule in an interesting way.

When to Use Light with the Rule of Thirds

•To balance asymmetrical compositions

•To guide the eye through a diagonal or horizontal movement

•To create a sense of flow, especially with light that enters from one side

•When you want your subject to feel anchored, but not static

Why This Will Make Your Photos Better

The Rule of Thirds is a time-tested way to make your photos feel balanced and intentional. When you combine it with the intentional use of light, you get compositions that don't just look good—they feel right. They have motion, energy, and mood.

You're not just placing a subject in the frame. You're composing with light as an equal player.

Quick Daily Practice

•Set your grid overlay to 3×3

•Photograph one subject in light positioned at:

   •Center

   •Top third

   •Side third

   •Corner intersection

•Compare the rhythm and flow of each composition

Final Thought

When you align subject and light with intention, your photographs start to resonate. The Rule of Thirds isn't just a guideline for where things go —it's a pathway for how light and subject dance within the frame.

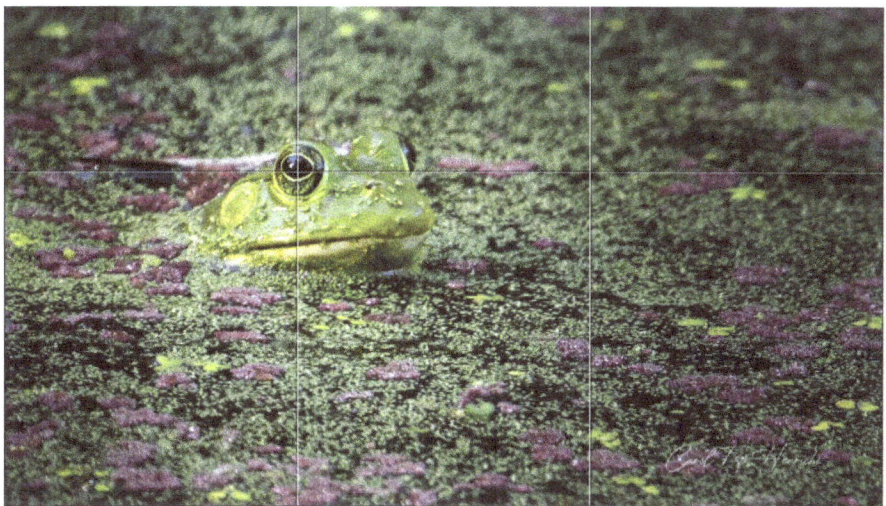

📌 Remember to use this as a guideline but not a hard and fast rule. In the end, you have to feel good about your photo—no necessarily anyone else does.

Day 20 Reflective Journal Pages

Use these prompts to reflect after each lesson or at the end of each week. There's no right or wrong way to answer—let your thoughts flow honestly and creatively.

Day 20: Light and the Rule of Thirds

1. What did I observe about the light today?

2. What surprised or challenged me during this lesson?

3. Which image felt the strongest—and why?

4. What would I do differently if I repeated this exercise?

5. Notes, thoughts, or ideas sparked today:

[Space for writing or sketching]

Day 21: Framing with Light and Shadow

"Light shows us what to see—shadow tells us where to look."

Why This Matters

Framing is a fundamental part of composition. It helps isolate your subject, lead the eye, and tell a clearer story. But you don't always need physical objects—like windows or arches—to create a frame. Light and shadow themselves can become frames, shaping your scene with invisible hands.

By using bright areas to highlight and darker areas to conceal, you can craft natural frames that are fluid, elegant, and often more emotionally resonant than anything physical. When you frame with light and shadow, you begin to sculpt the viewer's attention, focusing it with precision.

This approach brings depth, structure, and visual storytelling to your work.

What You'll Learn Today

- How to recognize and use light and shadow as natural framing tools
- How to position your subject within light "pools" or shadow "edges"
- How to use contrast to create isolation and emphasis
- How to compose images that feel layered, intimate, or dramatic

•

Key Concepts: What Is Light-Based Framing?

Framing with light and shadow involves intentionally placing your subject:

- •Inside a bright area, surrounded by darker tones (spotlight effect)

- •Emerging from the dark, like a figure in a shaft of sunlight

- •Against a shadow, so light defines the edges

- •Or behind a veil of light, like dappled sunlight through leaves

You're using contrast, not objects, to create a frame.

Step-by-Step Exercise: Framing with Light

Today, you'll explore a location (indoors or outdoors) and compose several images where light and shadow act as framing tools for your subject.

What You Need

- •DSLR or mirrorless camera

- •A subject (person, object, or scene)

- •A setting with strong directional light (e.g., window, spotlight, dappled shade, streetlight)

- •Aperture Priority or Manual mode

- •Optional: tripod, reflector

•

Step 1: Look for Natural Light Shapes

Walk through your home or a public space and look for:

- •Patches or pools of light on walls or floors
- •Light beams cutting through a room
- •Dark surroundings with one bright area
- •Overhead lights that isolate a tabletop or subject

Choose one of these light "frames" and place your subject inside the light, letting the shadows act as a soft border.

Step 2: Expose for the Highlight

- •Set your camera to Aperture Priority with f/2.8–f/5.6
- •Use exposure compensation (-1 to -2 EV) or meter from the highlight to keep the light area from blowing out
- •Let the shadows go deep—you're aiming for drama, not evenness

Step 3: Use Shadow as the Frame

Try the reverse:

- •Let the subject be partially or entirely in shadow
- •Use a bright background or edge of light to define the silhouette or shape

Place the subject just inside or next to a shadow line to suggest movement or emergence.

Step 4: Try Dappled or Filtered Light

Photograph a subject under:

- •Tree branches, window blinds, curtains, or lace

- Let patches of light create a frame within the frame—like a vignette or spotlight

- Use shallow depth of field to soften edges and focus attention

Capture at least one image that feels layered and intimate through patterned light.

Step 5: Review and Reflect

Compare your images and ask:

- Did light and shadow help contain or emphasize your subject?

- Where did the eye go first—and did it stay where you wanted it?

- Did you achieve a sense of intimacy, drama, or focus?

Note which framing technique felt most natural—and which challenged your creativity.

When to Use Light-Based Framing

- To create mood or mystery

- To highlight the subject without distractions

- To isolate a figure in a chaotic or busy setting

- To add visual interest with minimal props or clutter

Why This Will Make Your Photos Better

Framing with light and shadow trains your eye to see composition in tones, not just objects. It gives your images clarity and emotional weight—pulling the viewer in and holding their attention with purpose.

As you continue to refine this skill, your photos will feel more cinematic, clean, and visually confident.

Quick Daily Practice

•Find one strong light source today—window, lamp, or sunlight

•Place your subject in the light, then in the shadow

•Take 3 photos using light or dark as a frame

•Observe: Where does the light stop? Where does the viewer start to look?

Final Thought

Light carves the stage. Shadow closes the curtains. Together, they form a frame that's invisible to the untrained eye—but unforgettable in the final image. Learn to see the interplay, and you'll begin composing not just with subjects—but with space, silence, and light itself.

I could hardly believe it when this dove landed on the fence post and turned its head toward the light streaming in through the tree branches.This image of a White-winged Dove is a beautiful demonstration of how light and shadow can act as compositional tools, not just illumination. The bird is lit by soft, dappled light—filtered through the branches of a nearby tree—creating a natural frame of contrasting shadow around it. The interplay of light and dark draws the viewer's eye directly to the dove, emphasizing its form and expression while subtly obscuring the surrounding space. As we explored in Day 21, this technique uses light as a framing element, guiding focus without the need for physical borders. In this photo, the shadows create depth and intimacy, while the highlights gently sculpt the bird from its surroundings —transforming a quiet moment into a visually compelling image.

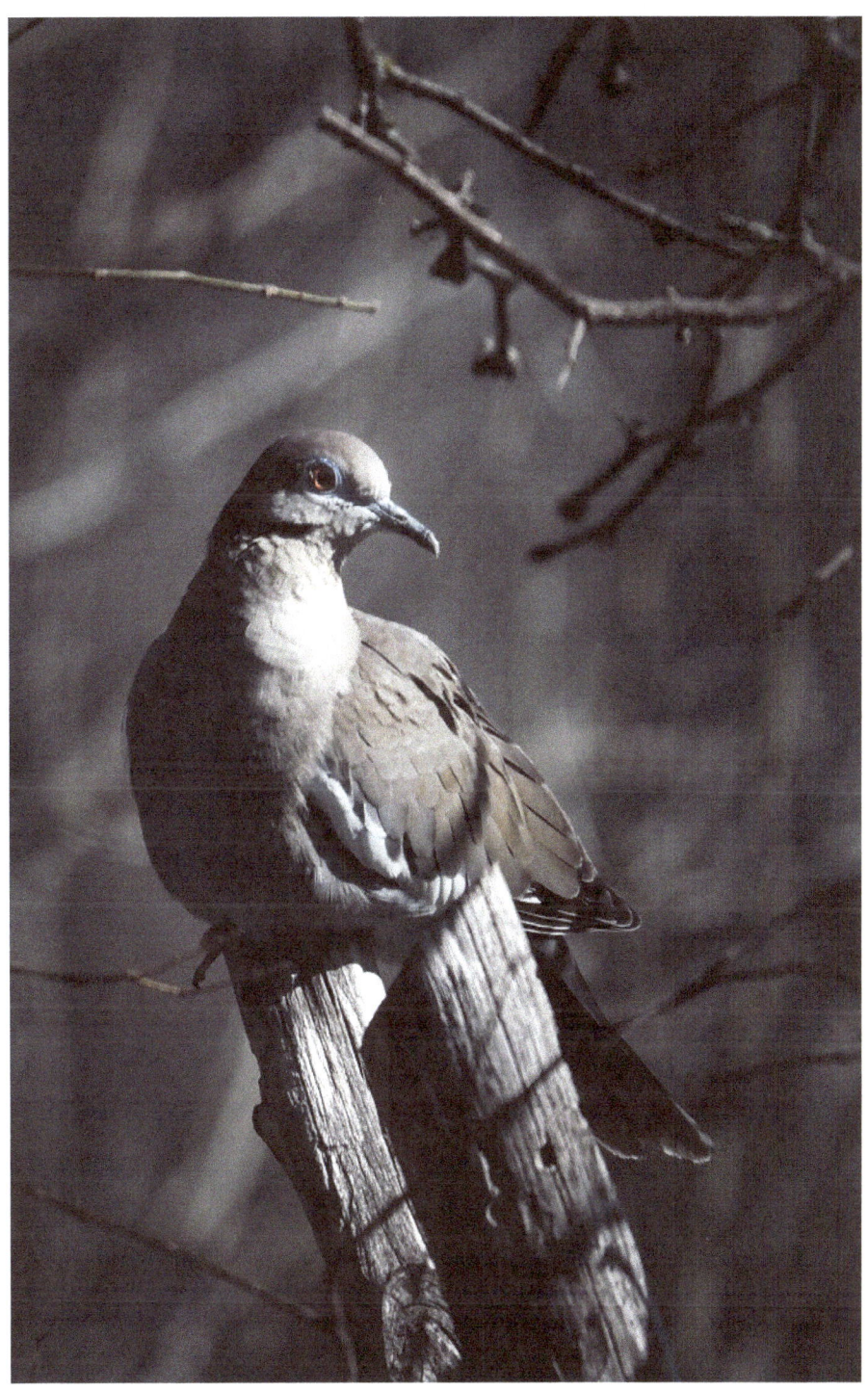

Day 21 Reflective Journal Pages

Use these prompts to reflect after each lesson or at the end of each week. There's no right or wrong way to answer—let your thoughts flow honestly and creatively.

Day 21: Framing with Light and Shadow

1. What did I observe about the light today?

2. What surprised or challenged me during this lesson?

3. Which image felt the strongest—and why?

4. What would I do differently if I repeated this exercise?

5. Notes, thoughts, or ideas sparked today:

[Space for writing or sketching]

Week 3 Reflection: Composition with Light

This week you began using light not just as a tool for exposure—but as a central part of your composition. You explored how to lead the eye, frame your subject, and evoke emotion using highlights, shadows, and direction. You saw how silhouettes can speak boldly, how soft window light can convey intimacy, and how framing with contrast can elevate a simple scene into something striking. These lessons asked you to be more intentional, to think in terms of story, not just subject. And in doing so, you've started shaping light with purpose. You're not just taking pictures —you're creating photographs that *feel* like something. Keep watching, keep composing, and keep listening to what your images are trying to say.

You explored how to use light not just for exposure—but as a compositional force. You learned to shape visual stories by placing your subjects in light, beside it, or defined by shadow. From bold silhouettes to quiet window-lit portraits, each lesson built your awareness of how light and dark direct the eye, set the mood, and clarify what matters in your frame.

You discovered how to:

- Simplify scenes using silhouettes and negative space

- Use shadows as subjects and compositional tools

- Work with soft, flattering window light for portraits

- Bounce and reflect light to balance contrast and lift shadows

- Combine light placement with the Rule of Thirds for dynamic compositions

- Frame your subjects using natural light and shadow

Now, you're no longer just seeing light—*you're composing with it*, using it to lead the eye, isolate your subject, and tell more intentional visual stories.

You've moved from capturing what's in front of you to crafting what the viewer sees and feels.

Week 4 Introduction: Creative Challenges

You've built a strong foundation—now it's time to stretch your vision.

Week 4 is about putting all your knowledge into practice through creative, hands-on challenges. Each day will ask you to step outside your comfort zone, think more playfully, or dig deeper into your unique photographic voice.

These challenges will help you:

- •Experiment with color, abstraction, and emotion

- •Explore new light scenarios like night photography and artificial light

- •Practice storytelling, repetition, minimalism, and visual poetry

- •Create mini photo series that reflect your growing skills and perspective

This is where you go beyond technique and begin to define your style. You'll be encouraged to slow down, observe with new eyes, and find light in unexpected places—even in the quiet or the ordinary.

You already know how to use your camera and how to read the light. Now let's create with purpose and make images that are truly your own.

Day 22: Minimal Light, Maximum Mood

"You don't need more light—just more intention."

Why This Matters

Some of the most powerful images are born not in abundance, but in restraint. When you limit your light source—whether by choice or necessity—you invite mood, intimacy, and tension into your frame. Minimal light forces you to simplify your composition and be intentional about what's revealed… and what's left in shadow.

Today's challenge helps you embrace low-light scenes not as problems to fix, but as opportunities to create atmosphere. You'll explore how darkness can enhance emotion, shape perception, and lead to more evocative storytelling.

What You'll Learn Today

- How to create dramatic mood using just one light source
- How to compose for emotion and intimacy in low light
- How to manage exposure and shadow intentionally
- How to work with minimal tools in low-light conditions

Key Concepts: Why Less Light Can Be More

In bright scenes, everything competes for attention. In dark ones, what's visible becomes precious. Minimal light:

- Adds mystery and drama

- Emphasizes contrast and texture

- Simplifies clutter and distractions

- Enhances mood, tone, and storytelling

By limiting your light, you allow your viewer to lean in, to engage with the image more deeply.

Step-by-Step Exercise: One Light, One Subject

You'll photograph a subject using just one light source, composing your scene to maximize contrast, shape, and mood.

What You Need

- DSLR or mirrorless camera

- One light source: a lamp, flashlight, phone light, or candle

- A subject with shape or texture (person, hands, book, object)

- Manual or Aperture Priority mode

- Tripod or steady surface (recommended)

Step 1: Set the Scene

Turn off all other lights. Choose a dark room or wait until evening. Position your subject in a way that only part of it is lit.

Try:

- A lamp at a 45° angle

- A flashlight pointed across the frame

- Candlelight for subtle glow

- Light through blinds or fabric for texture

Think cinematic: shadowy corners, a single beam, a hand lit in darkness.

Step 2: Compose for Mood

Use negative space and deep shadows to simplify your scene.

Try:

- •Placing your subject to one side, letting light fade into black
- •Isolating only part of the subject in the light (e.g., just the eyes, hands, or an edge)
- •Leaving the background completely dark

Use f/2.8 to f/5.6 for depth and softness. Expose for the light area—let the shadows go deep.

Step 3: Refine and Reflect

Take 3–5 variations:

- •Change the angle or height of your light
- •Let more or less of the subject enter the light
- •Try using a reflector or white card just slightly to lift the darkest shadows

As you shoot, ask: What mood am I creating? What emotion am I inviting?

Step 4: Review and Analyze

Look through your images and note:

- •Where your eye goes first—and why
- •Which parts of the image feel mysterious or emotional
- •Whether the light supports the mood or story you were after

Creative Prompts (Optional)

- •Photograph hands in low light—create a gesture or story through position alone

195

- Shoot an object that means something to you, lit by candlelight

- Capture a face in profile, mostly in shadow

- Use low-key lighting to turn a simple scene into a cinematic moment

---

Why This Will Make Your Photos Better

This challenge teaches restraint. It reminds you that what you leave out is as important as what you include. By working with minimal light, you strengthen your compositional instincts, sharpen your sense of drama, and learn to embrace the emotional power of shadow.

Your photos become less about information—and more about feeling.

Quick Daily Practice

- Turn off the lights in a room except for one small lamp or light

- Place a subject partially in the beam

- Take a single frame that tells a mood-driven story using minimal light

- Share it with a title or single word that captures the feeling

---

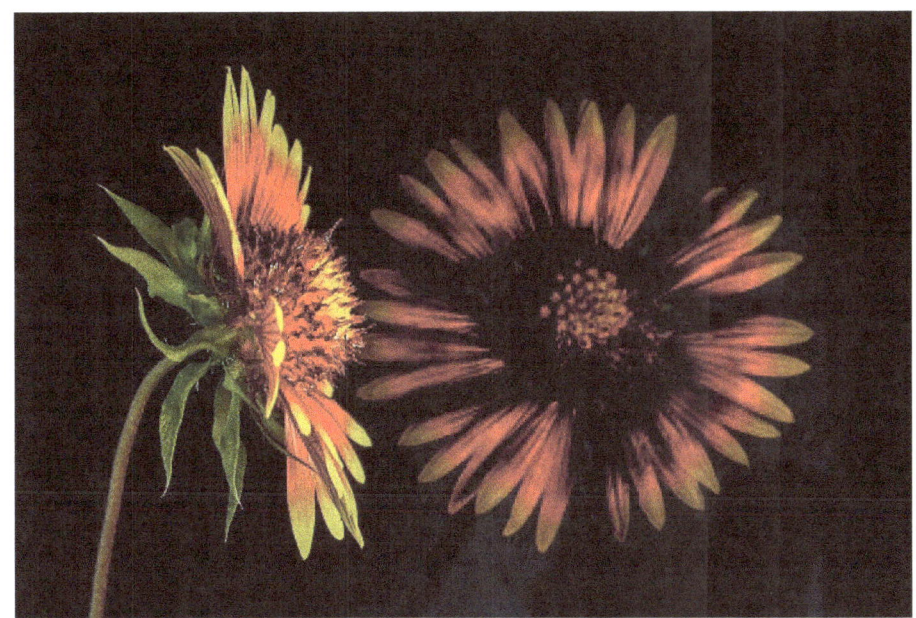

This photograph of a blanketflower was created using just one constant light source, positioned to gently illuminate the flower while allowing the rest of the scene to fall into darkness. A sheet of smooth black plastic served as the background—and cleverly, as a reflective surface, echoing the flower's form and adding depth without clutter. This image beautifully demonstrates the principles from Day 22: how minimal lighting, when placed with care, can create a strong focal point and a sense of quiet drama. The black backdrop isolates the subject, and the single light draws attention to its texture, color, and symmetry—proving that mood and visual impact don't require multiple lights or elaborate setups. Sometimes, just one well-placed light and a bit of reflection are all you need to let the subject shine.

Final Thought

Great photography doesn't always come from adding more—it often comes from revealing less. Light only where it's needed. Shadow where the imagination can roam.

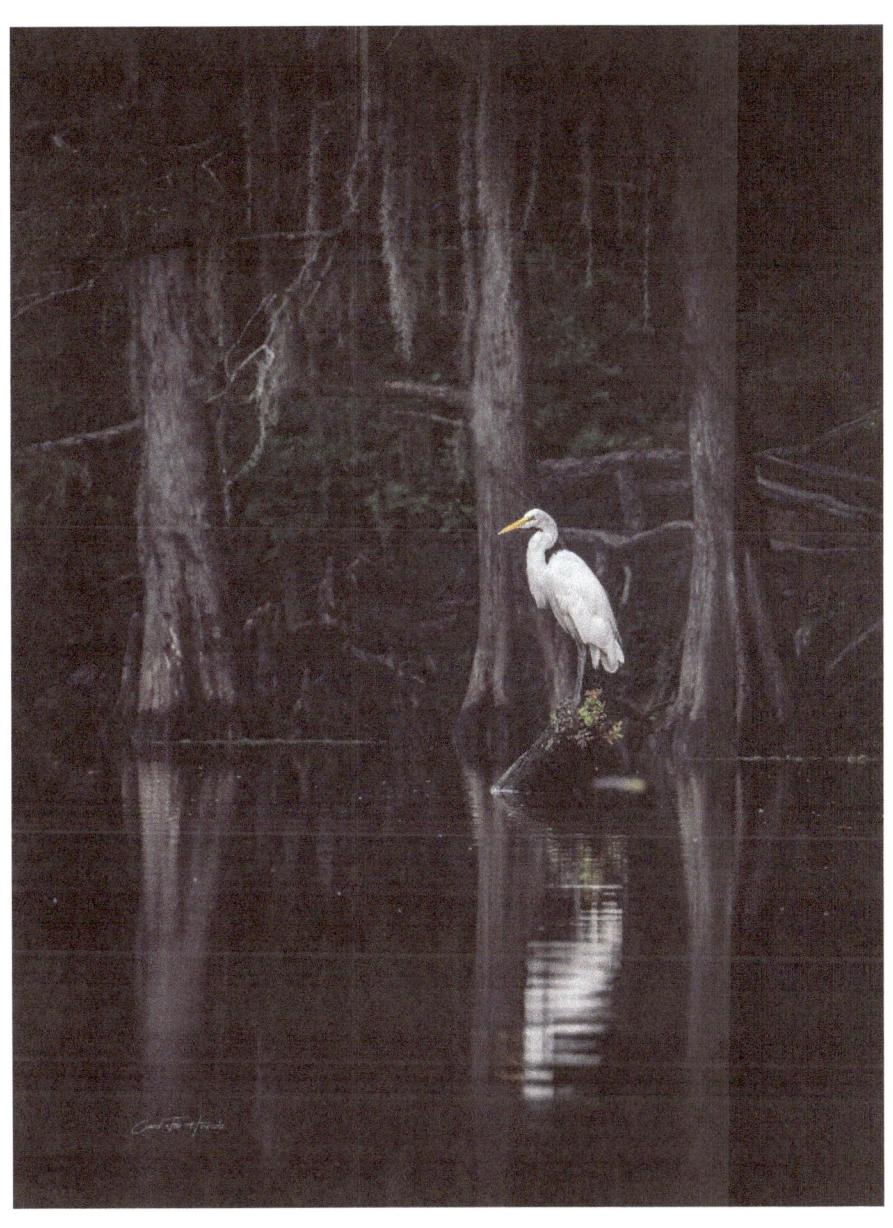

Day 22 Reflective Journal Pages

Use these prompts to reflect after each lesson or at the end of each week. There's no right or wrong way to answer—let your thoughts flow honestly and creatively.

Day 22: Minimal Light, Maximum Mood

1. What did I observe about the light today?

2. What surprised or challenged me during this lesson?

3. Which image felt the strongest—and why?

4. What would I do differently if I repeated this exercise?

5. Notes, thoughts, or ideas sparked today:

[Space for writing or sketching]

Day 23: Color of Light: Warm, Cool & Emotional

> "Light doesn't just illuminate—
> it speaks in tone, temperature, and feeling."

Why This Matters

All light has color—even if we don't always notice it. From the golden glow of candlelight to the icy tint of a snowy morning, the color temperature of light dramatically influences the emotion and mood of your images.

Understanding how to recognize, control, and use the color of light will help you make images that feel the way you want them to. It can warm a scene to feel nostalgic and cozy—or cool it down to feel detached and quiet. When used intentionally, light's color becomes a powerful emotional tool in your storytelling.

What You'll Learn Today

- •What color temperature is and how to identify it
- •The emotional impact of warm vs. cool lighting
- •How to use white balance settings creatively
- •How to mix light sources for unique moods

Key Concepts: Understanding Color Temperature

Light has color based on its temperature, measured in Kelvin (K):

Light Source	Color Temp	Feel
Candlelight	~1500K	Very warm, romantic, nostalgic
Tungsten lamp	~2800K	Warm, homey
Sunrise/Sunset	~3200–4000K	Golden, emotional
Midday sunlight	~5500K	Neutral, true-to-life
Cloudy/overcast	~6000–7000K	Cool, soft, moody
Shade or open sky	~7000–9000K	Very cool, quiet, detached

Step-by-Step Exercise: Creating Mood Through Color Temperature

Today, you'll shoot the same subject using different light sources or white balance settings to see how color of light shifts mood.

What You Need
- •DSLR or mirrorless camera
- •A subject (person, object, or still life)
- •Access to at least two types of light (window light, lamp, or LED)
- •White balance control (custom, preset, or Kelvin setting)

Step 1: Photograph in Warm Light

Use a lamp, candle, or sunset window light to illuminate your subject.
- •Set your white balance to Tungsten (Incandescent) or adjust manually to 3000–3500K to keep the warmth
- •Avoid neutralizing the color—you want to embrace the golden tones

•Take a few portraits or still life images

Observe the emotional tone: nostalgic, soft, romantic?

Step 2: Photograph in Cool Light

Now photograph the same subject using:

•Window light on a cloudy day

•Shade outdoors

•LED lights or blue-tinted bulbs

Set your white balance to Shade, Cloudy, or adjust manually to 6000–7500K to preserve the cool tones.

Does it feel quieter, more modern, maybe even a bit somber?

Step 3: Intentionally Shift White Balance

Photograph one subject:

•Once with a warm white balance setting (e.g., Cloudy or 6500K)

•Again with a cool white balance (e.g., Incandescent or 3000K)

Compare:

•Which version tells the story better?

•Did one feel off, or surprisingly effective?

■ This teaches you that white balance isn't just technical—it's emotional.

Step 4: Try Mixed Lighting (Optional)

Find a scene with two types of light—for example:

•A window and a lamp

•Sunlight and artificial light

•Two rooms with different bulbs

Capture how the mix of warm and cool creates tension, contrast, or unusual harmony.

Review and Reflect

Compare your warm, cool, and mixed images. Ask:

- •What emotions are evoked by each lighting style?

- •Did color change how you interpreted the scene?

- •How could you use this knowledge in portrait, travel, or fine art photography?

Tips for Controlling Color of Light

- •Use White Balance presets to match or intentionally shift the scene

- •In Manual mode, set Kelvin temperature for full control

- •Avoid mixing color temperatures unless it's a creative choice

- •Shoot in RAW so you can adjust white balance in post without damaging image quality

- •Let warmth amplify emotion; let coolness simplify and calm

Why This Will Make Your Photos Better

Light isn't just brightness—it's color, feeling, and context. When you learn to observe and use the color temperature of light, you move beyond capturing the scene—you start setting the tone.

This awareness will help you make stronger visual and emotional choices, whether you're photographing a joyful family gathering or a quiet morning landscape.

Quick Daily Practice

- •Photograph the same object using two different light sources (warm and cool)

•Take one neutral white balance shot and one intentionally colored
•Ask: Which one feels more like the story I want to tell?

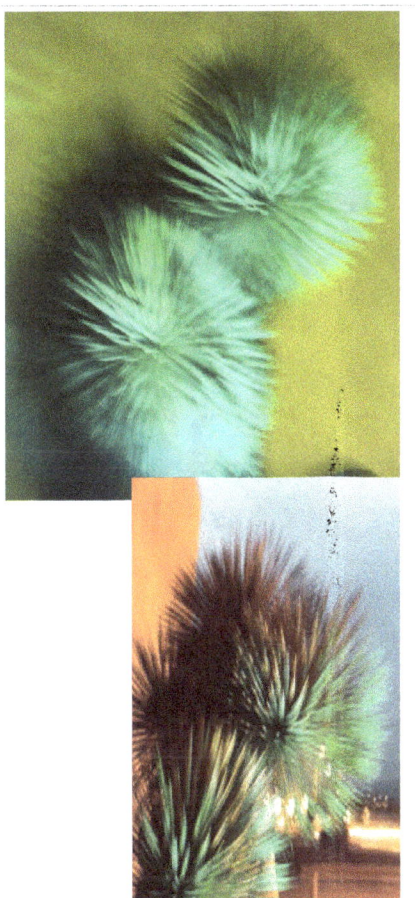

Both shots were captured using intentional camera movement but with different white balance settings.

These two photographs of the same yucca plant offer a powerful side-by-side demonstration of how white balance affects not just color, but emotion and atmosphere in an image. In the first version, a cool white balance renders the scene with bluish tones—giving the image a quiet, distant, almost serene mood. The green of the yucca appears more muted and the overall feeling is crisp and subdued. In contrast, the second image, captured with a warm white balance, infuses the scene with golden tones that create a sense of warmth, vitality, and intimacy. The plant appears sunlit and inviting, as if glowing from within.

As explored in Day 23, the color temperature of light—and how you choose to interpret it in-camera—has a direct impact on the emotional tone of your photograph. These two images of the same subject show how a simple shift in white balance can tell two entirely different stories, both visually compelling in their own way.

Final Thought

Light has a voice. Sometimes it whispers warmth. Sometimes it sings in blue. When you learn to hear its tone—and use it with care—your photographs begin to speak in color, and in emotion.

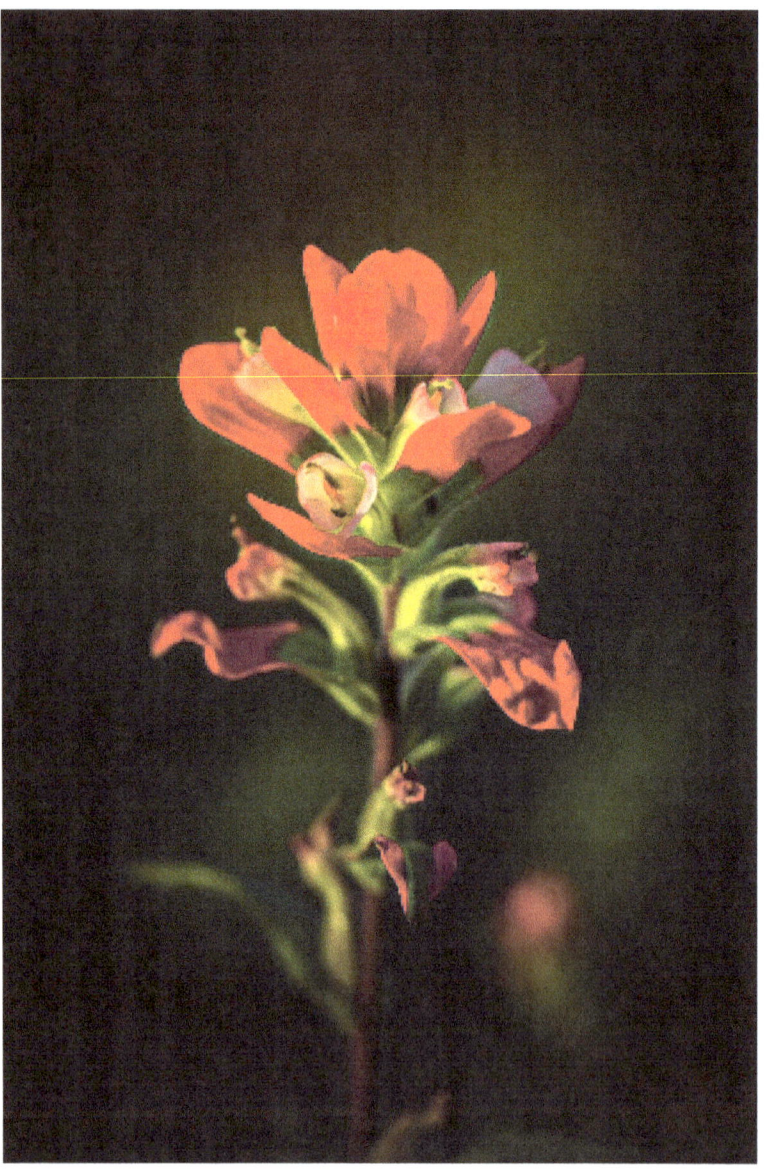

This photograph of an Indian Paintbrush, captured during sunset's golden hour, is a vivid example of how the color of light shapes the emotional tone of an image. The warm, amber light of the setting sun casts a rich glow across the flower, enhancing the reds and oranges in its petals and creating a sense of warmth, softness, and serenity. With the light coming from the side, the image gains depth and dimension—highlighting the texture of each bloom while casting gentle shadows that add form and contrast. Day 23 focuses on how warm and cool light influence mood, and this image fully embraces the golden hues of evening light to evoke a peaceful, almost nostalgic feeling. It's a perfect example of how light's color can not only define a subject but also shape the viewer's emotional response.

Day 23 Reflective Journal Pages

Use these prompts to reflect after each lesson or at the end of each week. There's no right or wrong way to answer—let your thoughts flow honestly and creatively.

Day 23: The Direction of LIght

1. What did I observe about the light today?

2. What surprised or challenged me during this lesson?

3. Which image felt the strongest—and why?

4. What would I do differently if I repeated this exercise?

5. Notes, thoughts, or ideas sparked today:

[Space for writing or sketching]

Day 24: Night Photography Without Flash

"The night has its own kind of light—quiet, rich, and full of mystery."

Why This Matters

Night photography opens up an entirely different visual world—but many new photographers shy away from it, assuming it requires complex gear or a flash. In reality, with a basic camera, a tripod, and a willingness to slow down, you can capture the soft glow of city lights, the depth of a moonlit landscape, or the story in a single streetlamp.

Working without flash teaches you to embrace ambient light, push your exposure skills, and get comfortable with long shutter speeds, high ISOs, and low-light composition.

Today's challenge encourages you to step outside after dark and discover what light still remains.

What You'll Learn Today

- •How to take sharp, well-exposed night photos without using flash
- •How to use long exposures and high ISO settings effectively
- •How to find and work with existing ambient light sources
- •How to reduce noise and motion blur in low-light conditions

Key Concepts: Working With Natural Night Light

When you shoot at night without flash, you're relying on available light sources like:

- •Streetlamps
- •Neon signs

- •Headlights
- •Window glow
- •Moonlight or reflected light

To make these usable, you must adjust:

- •ISO: Raise it (e.g., 1600–3200) to make the sensor more sensitive

- •Shutter speed: Slow it down (e.g., 1–10 seconds) to gather more light

- •Aperture: Open wide (e.g., f/1.8 to f/4) to let in as much light as possible

A tripod or sturdy surface becomes essential when working with slow shutter speeds.

Step-by-Step Exercise: Capture the Light That Remains

Tonight, you'll photograph a nighttime scene using only the light already present—no flash, no added lamps. You'll experiment with long exposures and high ISO settings to discover what your camera sees after dark.

What You Need

- •DSLR or mirrorless camera

- •A tripod or steady surface

- •Manual or Shutter Priority mode

- •Remote shutter release or self-timer (to avoid camera shake)

- •Scene with ambient light (street, building, porch, moonlit landscape)

Step 1: Set Up Your Scene

Choose a scene with at least one light source—a streetlamp, illuminated window, or even traffic lights. Make sure there's something of interest in the frame (building, tree, person, etc.).

Place your camera on a tripod or solid surface.

Step 2: Dial in Your Exposure Settings

Start with:

- •ISO: 1600 (or higher if needed)
- •Aperture: As wide as your lens allows (e.g., f/2.8)
- •Shutter speed: Start at 1 second and adjust longer if needed
- •Focus: Use manual focus if your camera struggles in low light

Take a test shot. Is it too dark? Try a slower shutter. Too noisy? Reduce ISO and lengthen shutter time.

Step 3: Experiment With Movement

- •Take a long exposure (5–10 seconds) and include moving lights (cars, bikes, or people).
- •Try capturing light trails from headlights or taillights.
- •Let motion blur tell a story—don't fight it.

For light trails: ISO 100–400, f/8, shutter speed 10–20 seconds.

Step 4: Capture Stillness and Mood

Photograph a quiet street corner, a house with a glowing window, or a statue under soft light.

Keep shadows deep. Let mood guide your composition.

Step 5: Review and Reflect

Look at your night shots and ask:

>•Were your exposures accurate—or too noisy or blurry?

>•Which settings gave you the clearest result?

>•Which images captured a feeling, not just a scene?

Note what light sources worked best and how you might frame differently next time.

Tips for Successful Night Photography Without Flash

>•Use a tripod to avoid blur from slow shutter speeds

>•Shoot in RAW for easier noise reduction and color correction

>•Use manual focus—your camera may struggle in the dark

>•Bracket exposures (take multiple versions at different settings)

>•Try exposing for the highlights, then bringing up the shadows in post-processing

Why This Will Make Your Photos Better

Night photography trains you to work with limited light and maximum intention. It slows you down and sharpens your eye. You begin to see light sources not just as illumination—but as atmosphere, path, and punctuation.

Shooting at night builds confidence in exposure, deepens your sense of composition, and adds an entire new chapter to your visual storytelling.

Quick Daily Practice

>•Go out after dark with your camera and tripod

•Choose one well-lit subject or street scene

•Take 3 photos: one short exposure, one long exposure, one with light trails

•Review them to see how time and light shape your results

Final Thought

The night isn't dark—it's dimly lit by stories waiting to be told. Once you learn how to photograph without flash, you'll find there's more light—and more beauty—out there than you ever realized.

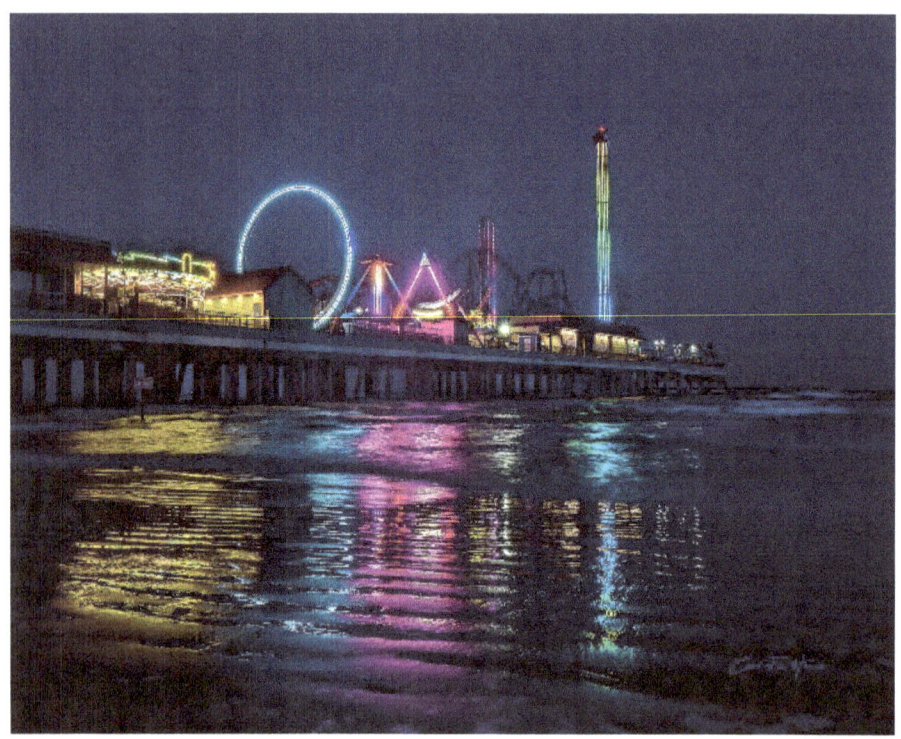

This nighttime photograph of Galveston's Pleasure Pier captures the vibrant glow of carnival lights shimmering against the dark sky—and dancing in colorful reflections across the wet sand and beach waters below. Taken without flash, the image embraces the ambient light of the scene, allowing the pier's neon and ride lights to become both subject and source of illumination. As taught in Day 24, night photography without flash requires balancing longer shutter speeds, wider apertures, and higher ISO settings to work with available light. This image does exactly that—preserving detail in the structure while allowing the rich colors and glowing reflections to create atmosphere and energy. The scene is lively, yet moody—a reminder that night light has its own magic, and that patience, a tripod, and intentional exposure can transform darkness into drama.

Day 24 Reflective Journal Pages

Use these prompts to reflect after each lesson or at the end of each week. There's no right or wrong way to answer—let your thoughts flow honestly and creatively.

Day 24: Night Photography Without Flash

1. What did I observe about the light today?

2. What surprised or challenged me during this lesson?

3. Which image felt the strongest—and why?

4. What would I do differently if I repeated this exercise?

5. Notes, thoughts, or ideas sparked today:

[Space for writing or sketching]

Day 25: Abstracting Reality with Light and Shadow

"When you stop showing what something is and start showing what it feels like—you're making art."

Why This Matters

Photography is often associated with realism—capturing what's in front of us clearly and accurately. But as a creative tool, the camera can also be used to distort, simplify, or reimagine reality, especially through light and shadow.

By focusing on patterns, shapes, tones, and textures rather than identifiable objects, you create abstract images that spark emotion, curiosity, and interpretation. Light and shadow become your raw materials—just like paint to a painter.

Today's challenge is to move beyond documentation and into abstraction, letting light guide your vision toward the unexpected.

What You'll Learn Today

- •How to use contrast, lines, and texture to create abstract compositions
- •How shadow and light can transform ordinary subjects
- •How to simplify reality by eliminating context
- •How to compose with mystery, rhythm, and emotion

Key Concepts: What Is Abstract Photography?

Abstract photography doesn't tell a literal story—it tells a visual one.

It relies on:

- •Strong light and deep shadow
- •Close-ups or unusual angles
- •Minimalism or repetition
- •Focus on shape, line, or contrast instead of subject identity

📌 The goal is to evoke, not explain.

Step-by-Step Exercise: Create an Abstract Using Light

Today you'll photograph an abstract image using light and shadow only, intentionally removing or obscuring the subject's identity.

What You Need

- •DSLR or mirrorless camera

- •A location with strong directional light (indoor window, late afternoon sun, flashlight)

- •Subjects with texture or geometry (fabrics, leaves, blinds, tools, glassware)

- •Manual focus (optional), Aperture Priority or Manual mode

Step 1: Hunt for Light and Form

Walk around your home or yard and look for how light hits surfaces—not the surfaces themselves.

- •Look for repeating lines from blinds or shadows on walls

- •Find textures (woodgrain, fabric, leaves) being enhanced by side light

- •Seek bright/dark juxtapositions where light cuts into shadow

Don't think about what the object is—look at what light is doing to it.

Step 2: Get Closer or Change Angles

To make the image abstract:

- Zoom in or move physically closer

- Shoot from above, below, or diagonally

- Fill the frame with texture, curve, or pattern

Avoid including recognizable edges or objects unless they support the abstraction.

Step 3: Play With Exposure and Focus

- Try underexposing to deepen shadows and enhance contrast

- Use shallow depth of field (f/2.8–f/4) to blur part of the image

- Try manual focus to highlight texture or create softness

Take 3–5 versions of the same subject, changing just one element at a time.

Step 4: Review and Reflect

Look at your images and ask:

- Can I tell what this is? Should I be able to?

- What feeling or rhythm does this image create?

- Did light and shadow help me hide or enhance key elements?

Choose one photo and give it a title based on feeling or idea, not subject (e.g., "Fractured," "Pulse," "Stillness").

Creative Prompts (Optional)

- Capture the shadow of something out of frame—only the light remains

- Photograph reflected light in distorted glass or metal

- Use a single shaft of light to illuminate just a curve or texture

- Create a composition with pure shape and tone

Why This Will Make Your Photos Better

Abstract work teaches you to see light more intuitively and less literally. It sharpens your understanding of shape, form, and contrast—skills that translate into all genres of photography.

Most importantly, abstraction frees you from rules. It gives you room to express, not just capture.

Quick Daily Practice

- Take 5 close-up shots today using light and shadow only
- Eliminate the object's identity—focus on shape, tone, or rhythm
- Choose one image and title it with a feeling or concept
- Post it without explaining what it is. Let others interpret it freely.

Final Thought

When you stop worrying about what your subject is and start focusing on how it feels, you unlock a new layer of creativity. Light and shadow become your poetry. Abstraction becomes your voice.

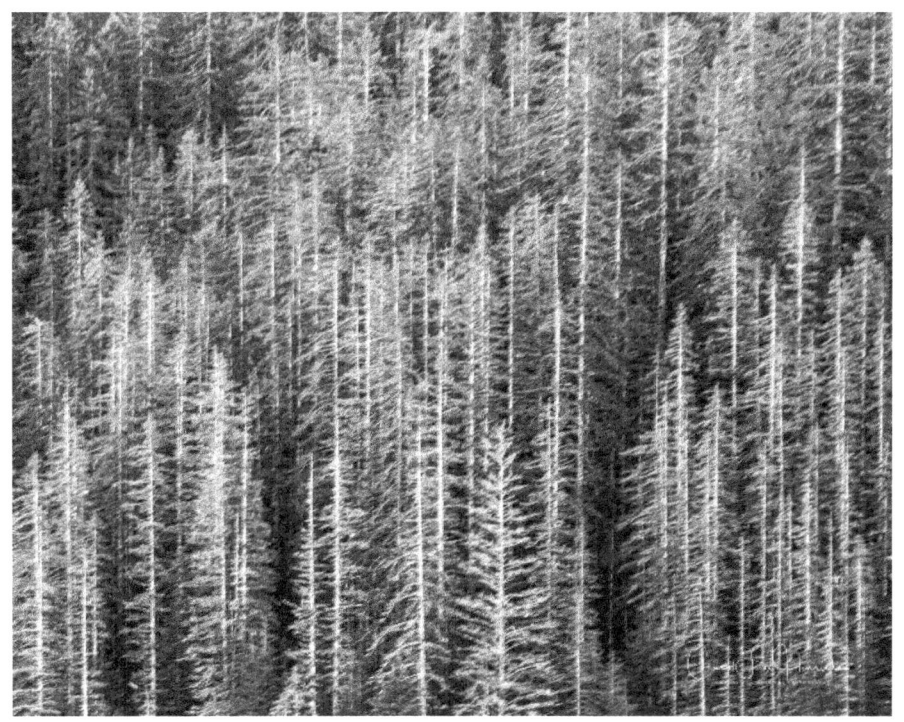

This photograph of a hillside densely covered in Sitka Spruce trees transforms a natural landscape into an almost abstract visual experience. The tightly packed trees create a strong pattern of repetition, with their pointed forms echoing rhythmically across the frame. Rather than focusing on a single subject, the image invites you to experience texture, structure, and visual flow. Converting the image to black & white removes the distraction of color and emphasizes the tonal contrasts between light and shadow—highlighting the natural geometry of the forest. As taught in Day 25, abstraction in photography often comes from reducing reality to its shapes, tones, and patterns, and this image does just that. It's not just a photo of trees—it's a study in rhythm, form, and how light reveals structure in nature.

Day 25 Reflective Journal Pages

Use these prompts to reflect after each lesson or at the end of each week. There's no right or wrong way to answer—let your thoughts flow honestly and creatively.

Day 25: Abstracting Reality with Light and Shadow

1. What did I observe about the light today?

2. What surprised or challenged me during this lesson?

3. Which image felt the strongest—and why?

4. What would I do differently if I repeated this exercise?

5. Notes, thoughts, or ideas sparked today:

[Space for writing or sketching]

Day 26: Visual Storytelling with a Single Light Source

"One light. One subject. One story told with intention."

Why This Matters

In photography, storytelling isn't just about subject—it's about how light reveals emotion, tension, or meaning. Using a single light source challenges you to create clarity, drama, or intimacy without distraction. It's minimalism with a purpose.

With only one light, you have to think more intentionally: Where should the eye go? What mood do I want? What stays hidden? This constraint sharpens your creative instincts and strengthens your visual voice.

Today's challenge is to use a single light source—natural or artificial—to craft a story in a single frame.

What You'll Learn Today

- •How to direct a viewer's attention with just one light source
- •How to create mood and narrative through selective lighting
- •How to simplify a scene to enhance storytelling impact
- •How shadow placement supports tension, mystery, or emotion

•

Key Concepts: One Light, One Intent

One light source creates:

- •Focused attention — the eye follows the light
- •High contrast — bold shadows define emotion or form
- •Mood and simplicity — no filler, just essentials
- •Greater control — you decide exactly what gets revealed

📌 When light is limited, your choices carry more weight.

Step-by-Step Exercise: Tell a Story with One Light

You'll build a scene (portrait, object, or moment) using a single light source to create a deliberate story or emotional response.

What You Need

- •DSLR or mirrorless camera
- •One light source: window, lamp, flashlight, candle, or phone
- •A subject (person, object, or still life with emotional resonance)
- •Tripod or steady surface
- •Optional: black foam core or backdrop to control reflections

•

Step 1: Choose a Story or Feeling

Decide what emotion or story you want to convey:

- •Solitude

- •Tension

- •Comfort

- •Nostalgia

- •Anticipation

- •Stillness

📌 Don't just light a subject—light a moment.

Step 2: Place Your Light Source

Position your subject in a dark or neutral environment, then introduce a single light.

Try:

- •Side light for depth and drama

- •Top-down light for mystery or anonymity

- •Backlight for silhouette and emotional distance

- •Low-angle light for suspense or storytelling tension

Use f/2.8–f/4 for shallow depth, or f/5.6+ for more detail.

Step 3: Compose and Control the Frame

Simplify:

- •Remove clutter that doesn't serve the story

- •Let part of the subject fall into shadow

- •Use negative space to increase mood or focus

Use manual exposure to preserve the highlights and let shadows stay rich.

Step 4: Experiment and Refine

Take several frames:

- •Slightly shift the angle or distance of the light
- •Adjust exposure to deepen shadows or pull out faint detail
- •Try moving the subject closer or farther from the light

After each change, ask: Does this help tell the story better?

Step 5: Review and Reflect

Look at your final images. Consider:

- •Does the light focus attention where you want it to?
- •Is the mood or story clear and intentional?
- •Did you leave space for the viewer to feel or interpret?

Give your favorite photo a title that reflects the mood or message.

Creative Prompts (Optional)

- •A pair of worn shoes lit by a window: A journey remembered
- •A cup and steam rising in a dark kitchen: Quiet morning
- •A face half-lit, looking away: Unspoken
- •A child's toy under a desk lamp: Forgotten

The goal: evoke a feeling with just light, shadow, and subject.

Why This Will Make Your Photos Better

When you can say more with less, your work becomes more powerful. Using a single light source teaches discipline, vision, and clarity. You stop relying on chance—and start crafting your scenes with intention.

And that's the heart of compelling photography: not just what you shoot, but how you choose to light it.

Quick Daily Practice

- In a dark or dim room, light one object or scene with a lamp or flashlight

- Take 3 photos:

  - One with dramatic shadows

  - One with soft, directional light

  - One with just a sliver of light

- Title the image that tells the strongest story

Final Thought

You don't need more light—you need more awareness of what light can say. When used with purpose, even the smallest lamp can illuminate a world of feeling.

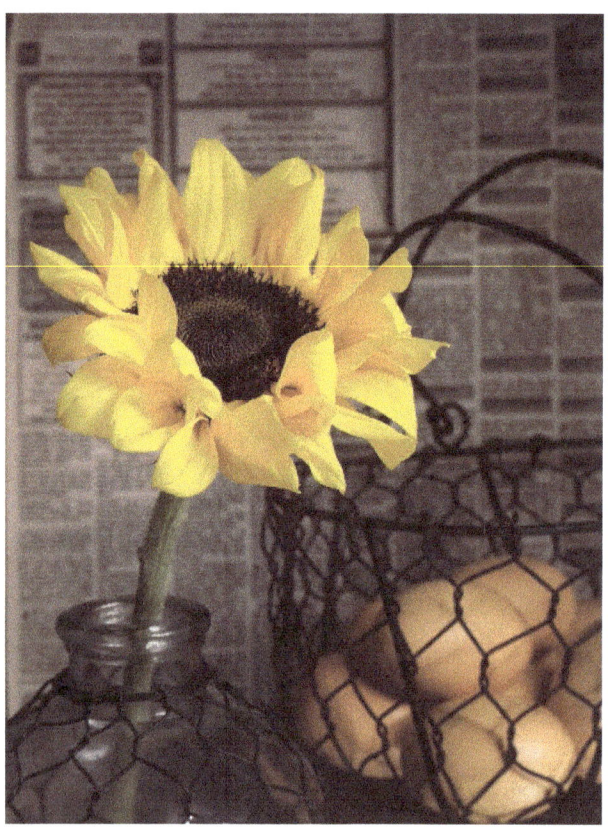

This still life photograph, with a sunflower in a chicken wire-covered vase, a basket of eggs, and a newspaper backdrop, tells a quiet, rustic story using just one carefully placed light source. The light is focused on the sunflower, casting gentle highlights across the petals while allowing the surrounding elements to fall gradually into shadow. This selective lighting creates a natural focal point, guiding the viewer's eye and adding a sense of narrative intimacy to the scene. The choice of elements evokes a farmstead setting—yet the single light adds mood and depth, suggesting memory, stillness, and time. As explored in Day 26, visual storytelling isn't about complexity—it's about using light with intention. This image shows how even the simplest materials, lit with care, can come together to tell a complete, evocative story in one frame.

Day 26 Reflective Journal Pages

Use these prompts to reflect after each lesson or at the end of each week. There's no right or wrong way to answer—let your thoughts flow honestly and creatively.

Day 26: Visual Storytelling with a Single Light Source

1. What did I observe about the light today?

2. What surprised or challenged me during this lesson?

3. Which image felt the strongest—and why?

4. What would I do differently if I repeated this exercise?

5. Notes, thoughts, or ideas sparked today:

[Space for writing or sketching]

Day 27: Using Light with Everyday Transparent Objects

"Even the simplest object becomes extraordinary when seen in the right light."

Why This Matters

We often overlook the visual potential of everyday items. But when light interacts with glass, plastic, or sheer materials, it can produce luminous colors, shadows, and reflections that elevate simple objects into subjects of visual interest. This exercise teaches you to see beauty in the ordinary —and how light reveals it.

What You'll Learn Today

•How light behaves when it passes through or reflects off transparent or translucent surfaces

•How to observe and photograph light refraction, glow, and color distortion

•How to make creative images using simple items you already have

Key Concepts

•Translucent vs. Transparent: Translucent objects scatter light (frosted glass, sheer fabric), while transparent ones let it pass through clearly (a drinking glass, clear water).

•Refraction: Light bends when it passes through materials of different densities—this can create rainbows, distortions, or magnified patterns.

•Backlighting: Placing your object between you and a light source can highlight its glow or create a silhouette with details glowing at the edges.

Step-by-Step Exercise: Visual Stories Photographing Through Objects

You'll create an image that conveys a feeling by shooting through an object.

What You Need

- •DSLR or mirrorless camera

- •One light source: window, lamp, flashlight, candle, or phone

- •A subject (person, object, or still life with emotional resonance)

- •Transparent and/or translucent items

- •Tripod or steady surface

Step 1: Find Your Object:

- Look for a see-through or semi-transparent item—glassware, water bottles, sheer curtains, cellophane, plastic wrappers, etc.

- Find an item to serve as your subject. I often use a flower in a vase for this.

Jot down your intention: What do I want this image to say or feel like?

Step 2: Choose a Light Source:

- Use natural light from a window or sunlight on a table.

- Add a flashlight or desk lamp if you want to control direction.

Step 3: Set It Up:

- Place the object where light can pass through it.

- Rotate it to find angles that create interesting effects.

- Observe First: Look closely. Where do you see reflections? Does the light create color or bend shapes?

Step 4: Start Shooting:

- Photograph from different distances and perspectives.

- Try zooming in to focus on distortion or details.

Step 5: Add Variation (Optional):

- Try placing something inside the object (a flower in a jar, beads in a bowl), or adding a few drops of water to catch extra light.

Why This Will Make Your Photos Better

This exercise improves your eye for subtle light behavior. You'll learn to recognize how everyday materials affect light—and how to use that knowledge to turn common subjects into artistic photos. It builds your ability to compose with intention and notice small details that can make a big visual impact.

One of my favorite ways to create moody, evocative flower photos is by shooting *through* surrounding plants. Instead of framing the flower in clear, open view, I often look for ways to partially obscure it using leaves, stems, or nearby grasses. When I position myself so that bits of foliage sit between my lens and the flower, it creates a soft, almost secretive feeling —like you've stumbled upon something quiet and beautiful. Use a wide aperture, like f/2.8 or f/4, to blur those foreground elements into gentle shadows or painterly color streaks.

I especially enjoy using this technique in the early morning or during golden hour, when the light is soft and directional. Backlighting can give petals a magical glow, while sidelight helps define texture and mood.

Sometimes I underexpose just slightly to enhance the shadows and keep the tone subdued. This approach helps me tell a quieter, more intimate story with my images—and reminds me that what we see through can be as important as what we see clearly.

Quick Daily Practice

- Spend 5–10 minutes photographing light through or on a different object.
- Try a wine glass, a window screen, a soap bubble, or a piece of wax paper.
- Watch how the light changes depending on the time of day.

Final Thought

Today's lesson invited you to look closer at the familiar. By holding space for quiet observation and thoughtful light, you created something unexpected from an object that might otherwise go unnoticed. Photographers who master light can make magic from the mundane. Today's exercise is a gentle reminder that beauty doesn't always come from exotic places—it often glows right on your windowsill.

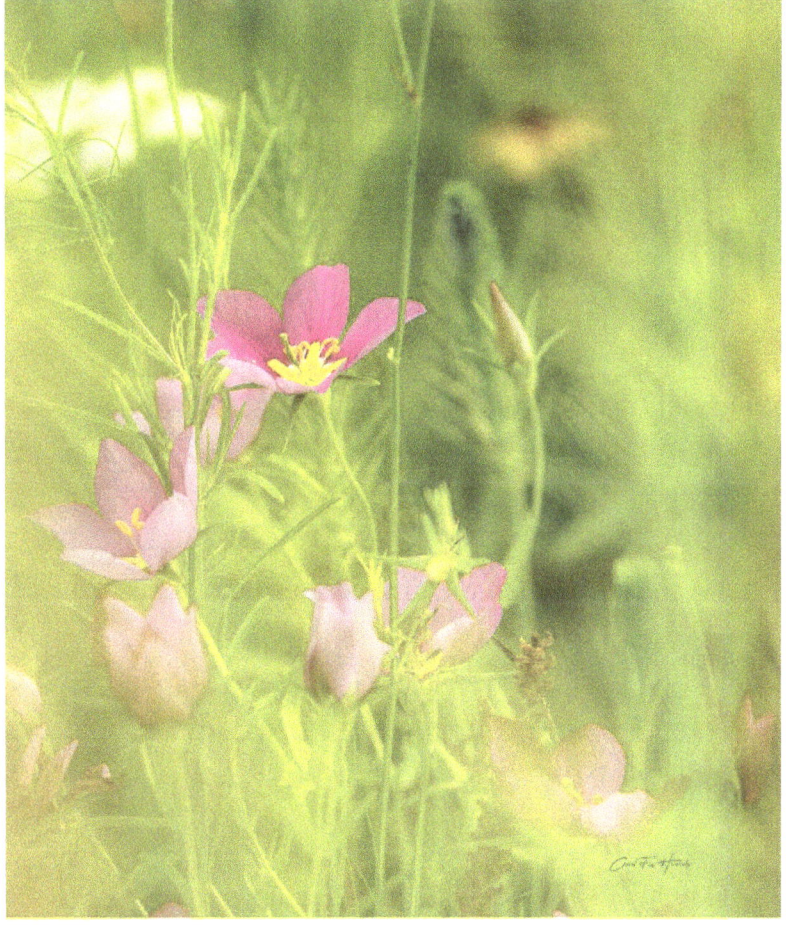

Day 27 Reflective Journal Pages

Use these prompts to reflect after each lesson or at the end of each week. There's no right or wrong way to answer—let your thoughts flow honestly and creatively.

Day 27: Using Light with Everyday Transparent Objects

1. What did I observe about the light today?

2. What surprised or challenged me during this lesson?

3. Which image felt the strongest—and why?

4. What would I do differently if I repeated this exercise?

5. Notes, thoughts, or ideas sparked today:

[Space for writing or sketching]

Day 28: Light and Repetition

"Repetition builds rhythm—and light sets the beat."

Why This Matters

Repetition is one of the most powerful (yet underrated) compositional tools in photography. It draws the viewer in with patterns, harmony, and rhythm. When paired with intentional lighting, repetition becomes even more compelling—revealing structure, disrupting uniformity, or adding subtle drama.

Repetition can soothe or surprise, depending on how the light interacts with it. Today's challenge helps you recognize repeated forms in the world around you—and use light to emphasize or break the pattern in creative ways.

What You'll Learn Today

- How to identify and photograph patterns and repeated elements
- How lighting can enhance, interrupt, or reveal repetition
- How to break a pattern with light to add tension or emphasis
- How to compose with rhythm for visual flow

Key Concepts: Light as a Pattern Partner

Repetition in photography shows up in:

- Architecture (windows, columns, tiles)
- Nature (leaves, petals, tree trunks)

•Everyday life (chairs, fence posts, utensils, shadows)

And light interacts with repetition in three key ways:

1.Enhancing it – evenly lit scenes highlight the uniformity

2.Interrupting it – selective light draws attention to a break in the pattern

3.Creating it – light itself becomes the repetition (e.g. window light casting striped shadows)

📌 Repetition calms the eye—contrast wakes it up.

Step-by-Step Exercise: Discover and Direct Repetition

Today, you'll find repeated forms or patterns and use light to emphasize, disrupt, or echo those repetitions in an image.

What You Need

•DSLR or mirrorless camera

•A location with patterns: building façade, bookshelf, staircase, picket fence, etc.

•A strong directional light source (natural or artificial)

•Optional: tripod for framing consistency

Step 1: Identify a Pattern

Walk around your environment and look for repetition in:

•Shapes (circles, squares, arches)

•Objects (bottles, slats, tools)

•Shadows (cast by blinds, leaves, or railings)

Find a subject where at least 3 or more elements repeat clearly.

Step 2: Compose for Rhythm

Frame your shot so the repeated elements:

- •Fill the frame for immersion

- •Lead the eye across or into the image

- •Emphasize geometry or symmetry

Try composing both horizontally and vertically.

Step 3: Use Light to Enhance or Disrupt

Now, work the light intentionally:

- •Let light fall evenly to show the full pattern

- •OR selectively light one part of the pattern to draw focus

- •Try casting shadows that repeat alongside the objects

- •Shoot during golden hour or side-lighting to add texture and depth

Optional: Use a flashlight or lamp to highlight just one piece of the pattern, creating tension or a visual "break."

Step 4: Review and Reflect

Compare your shots:

- •Did the repetition feel calm or energized?

- •Did light help reveal or interrupt the pattern?

- •Was there a clear focal point—or did the eye wander?

Choose one image and write a short caption or title that reflects its mood or rhythm (e.g., "Order Restored," "One Stands Apart").

Creative Prompts (Optional)

- •Photograph a row of identical objects, then remove or light just one differently

- •Capture repeating light patterns, like blinds or shadows across a wall

- •Find natural repetition (e.g., leaf clusters) and backlight them to reveal structure

- •Use a mirror or reflection to artificially repeat a subject

---

Why This Will Make Your Photos Better

Repetition trains your eye to see structure and balance in everyday scenes. Adding intentional lighting pushes you further—inviting you to create depth, contrast, or emotion in what could otherwise be flat. You'll start composing with more rhythm and clarity, making images that are both visually satisfying and creatively rich.

Quick Daily Practice

- •Find any repeating pattern in your environment

- •Take 3 photos: one with even light, one with selective light, one with strong shadow

- •Ask: Which version feels most alive? Which version feels most controlled?

Final Thought

Repetition builds the frame—but light tells the story. Whether you follow the pattern or break it, what matters is the rhythm you create for the eye to follow. And in that rhythm, there's the start of something uniquely yours.

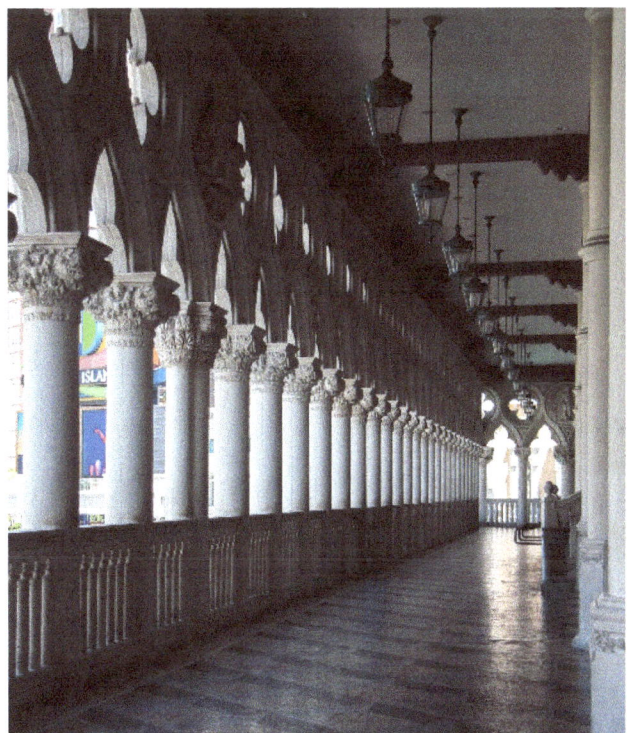

Two photos from Las Vegas NV illustrating how light accentuates patterns in architecture.

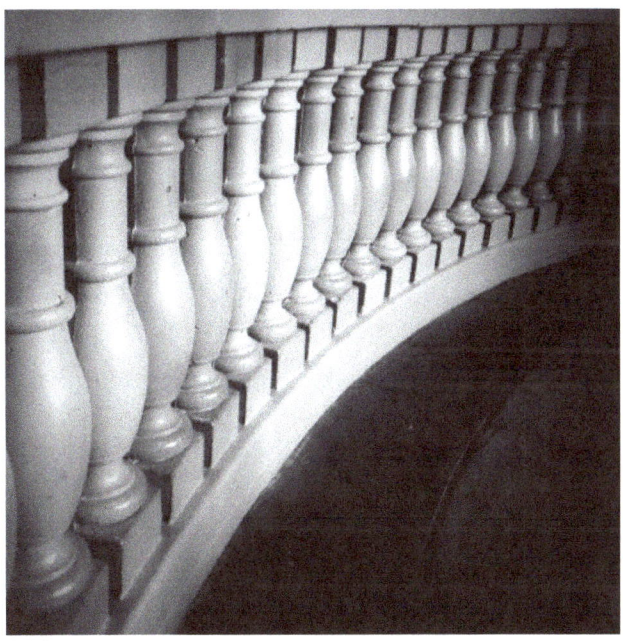

Day 28 Reflective Journal Pages

Use these prompts to reflect after each lesson or at the end of each week. There's no right or wrong way to answer—let your thoughts flow honestly and creatively.

Day 28: The Direction of LIght

1. What did I observe about the light today?

2. What surprised or challenged me during this lesson?

3. Which image felt the strongest—and why?

4. What would I do differently if I repeated this exercise?

5. Notes, thoughts, or ideas sparked today:

[Space for writing or sketching]

Day 29: Finding Light in Unlikely Places

"Beautiful light isn't rare—it's often just overlooked."

Why This Matters

It's easy to think great light only exists during golden hour, beside a big window, or under perfect conditions. But truthfully, great light can be found in the most unexpected places—you just have to learn to see it.

When you train your eye to recognize reflected glows, hidden sources, or fleeting flashes, you begin to photograph with curiosity and presence. You stop waiting for the light and start looking for it—everywhere.

This exercise is about sharpening your awareness. It's about letting go of the idea that light must be ideal to be interesting, and instead embracing light that is odd, fleeting, imperfect, or strangely beautiful.

What You'll Learn Today

- How to become more aware of unusual or hidden light sources
- How to recognize beauty in imperfect or mixed light
- How to compose quickly and creatively when light appears unexpectedly
- How to use any light—no matter how strange—to your advantage

Key Concepts: Unlikely Light Sources

Some of the most fascinating light appears when we least expect it:

- A glow from an open fridge

- A reflection off a metallic surface

- Colored light from a TV, laptop, or neon sign

- A sliver of sun through a crack in the curtain

- Car headlights, alleyway lights, or under-table lighting

- Shadows on the ceiling, bouncing from a glass of water

📌 These sources often feel unimportant until you slow down. Let them show you what they can do.

Step-by-Step Exercise: Go on a Light Hunt

Today, you'll spend 20–30 minutes exploring your surroundings to find at least 3 unexpected sources of light—then use one to make a photo.

What You Need

- DSLR or mirrorless camera (or smartphone if you're scouting casually)
- A curious eye and open mind
- Optional: object or subject to include in the scene

Step 1: Go Exploring

Look for places you might normally ignore:

- The inside of closets
- Bathrooms with colored tiles
- Reflections on kitchen counters
- The light between parked cars
- Under beds, behind curtains, in alleyways

Your goal isn't to take a perfect photo—it's to notice the light first.

Step 2: Identify 3 Light Sources

Once you start looking, you'll find them:

- A weird reflection?

- A surprisingly beautiful shadow?
- A warm sliver of artificial light?

Take snapshots of each, even if the scene doesn't feel fully formed.

Step 3: Choose One and Compose Intentionally

Pick the most interesting of the three light sources and ask:

- What story or emotion could I tell with this?
- What subject would belong in this light?
- How can I compose so the light leads the image?

Photograph it like it matters—because it does.

Step 4: Embrace the Imperfect

Unlikely light may come with:

- Mixed color temperatures
- Harsh shadows
- Strange angles
- Cluttered backgrounds

Instead of fixing these, work with them. Let them shape the image's character.

📌 Imperfect light often creates more authentic, edgy, or memorable photos.

Step 5: Review and Reflect

Ask yourself:

- What surprised you most about where you found light?

- Did working with weird or "bad" light unlock new creativity?

- How did you adapt your technique or expectations?

■ Write one sentence that begins with: "I didn't expect the light to…"

Creative Prompts (Optional)

- Light from inside a car at night

- A mirror catching light from a moving vehicle

- TV glow illuminating a still life or pet

- Streetlight shadows filtered through a chain-link fence

- Reflected color from stained glass or plastic

Why This Will Make Your Photos Better

Photographers who wait for perfect light miss a thousand moments a day. But photographers who learn to work with what is—and see beauty in the unexpected—develop resilience, originality, and a style that's truly their own.

This challenge is about trusting your eye and letting light surprise you.

Quick Daily Practice

- •Set a timer for 30 minutes

- •Walk through your home or neighborhood looking only for unusual light

- •Take at least 3 snapshots

- •Choose one and make a final image with intention

- •Post it with the caption: "Light found, not staged."

Using Light Painting for Day 29: Finding Light in Unlikely Places

Day 29 encourages photographers to look beyond the obvious and discover how light—especially unusual or overlooked sources—can be used creatively. Light painting is a perfect extension of this lesson, because it teaches you to become the creator of the light, not just the observer.

Light painting involves using a handheld light source, such as a flashlight, phone, or LED wand, to selectively illuminate parts of a scene during a long exposure. This allows you to literally paint with light in dark or low-light environments, revealing hidden details, guiding the viewer's eye, or adding surreal highlights where no light naturally exists.

Here's how it reinforces the Day 29 mindset:

•Reveals beauty in darkness: Like Day 29's emphasis on unusual or scarce light, light painting teaches you that the absence of light isn't a limitation—it's a blank canvas.

•Emphasizes creative control: Instead of relying on available light, you create your own, encouraging exploration and invention—both key values in Day 29's challenge.

•Highlights unexpected textures and forms: By lighting selective parts of a scene, you call attention to surfaces, objects, or emotions that might otherwise go unnoticed.

•Encourages experimentation: Just like Day 29 asks you to search and adapt, light painting rewards trial and error, patience, and curiosity.

A light-painted image feels like a secret revealed—something discovered through effort, imagination, and intentional observation. It's a natural evolution of what Day 29 begins: finding light where others don't even think to look.

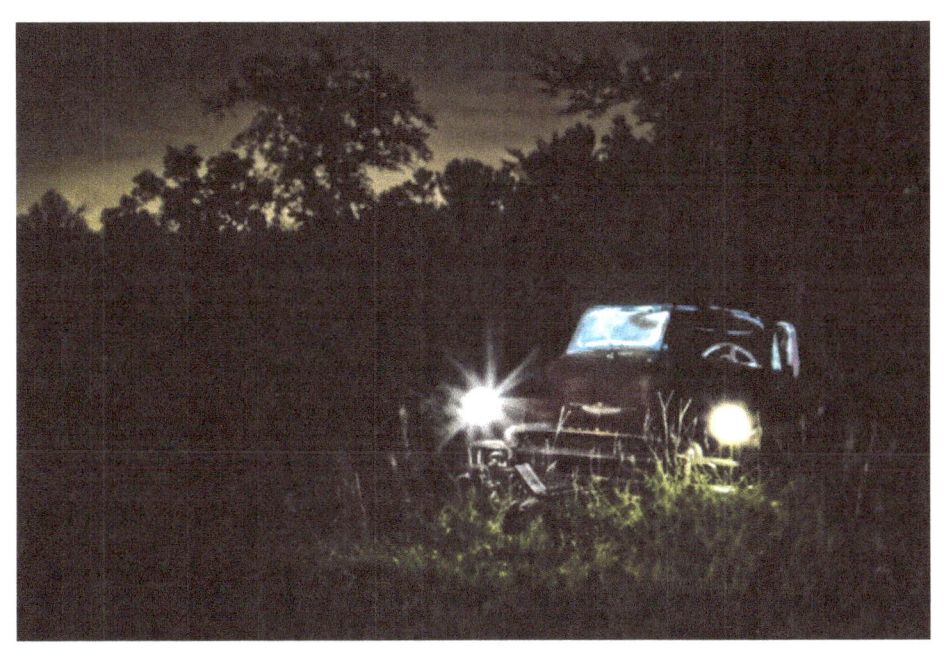

Bonus Lesson: Painting with Light

"When the light isn't there—make your own."

Why This Matters

In earlier lessons, we've practiced observing and shaping natural and artificial light. Light painting takes that one step further: it puts the power of light directly into your hands. Instead of waiting for ideal conditions, you become the source—adding light where it's needed, guiding the viewer's focus, and revealing surprising beauty in the dark.

Light painting invites you to embrace total creative control and explore scenes in a new way. It's not just a technical trick—it's a form of storytelling in darkness.

What You'll Learn Today

- How to create images using a handheld light source and long exposure
- How to selectively light a subject for drama or detail
- How to explore texture, form, and mood in total darkness
- How light painting supports the mindset of finding light in unlikely places

What You'll Need

- DSLR or mirrorless camera
- A tripod or stable surface (essential!)
- A flashlight, LED wand, or headlamp
- Remote shutter release or camera self-timer
- A completely dark environment (indoors or outdoors at night)

Step-by-Step Exercise: Painting with Light

Step 1: Choose Your Scene

Start with a simple still life, sculpture, flower, or found object. Outdoors, you might light paint a tree, rock, or even an old building. Total darkness or very low light is key.

Step 2: Set Your Exposure

Use Manual mode and start with these base settings:

- Shutter speed: 10 to 30 seconds
- Aperture: f/5.6 or f/8
- ISO: 100 to 400

Focus manually or use a flashlight to assist auto-focus, then switch to manual to lock it in.

Step 3: Begin Painting

- Trigger the shutter and move your light source across the subject slowly and intentionally
- Try lighting only parts of the subject to create contrast
- Move steadily to avoid hotspots or unintentional streaks
- You can use snoots, colored gels, or your hand to shape or filter the light

Repeat and experiment. You'll likely need several tries to find the right rhythm and coverage.

Creative Variations

•Use a colored flashlight or gel for a surreal mood

•Light from behind the subject for dramatic outlines

•Paint the background separately to create depth

•Try writing or drawing in the air with light for more experimental results

Review and Reflect

Look at your image and ask:

•What part of the image does the light guide your eye to first?

•How does painting light change the mood compared to traditional lighting?

•What surprises did you discover in the dark?

Why This Will Make Your Photos Better

Light painting trains your creative instincts—it forces you to slow down, plan your light intentionally, and think like a visual sculptor. It reinforces everything you've learned about how light shapes emotion, directs focus, and reveals form.

It's also just fun. The kind of fun that reminds you why you picked up a camera in the first place.

Quick Practice

•Set up a still life in a dark room

•Try 3 variations: lighting from above, side, and behind

•Use your light like a brush—and let your subject emerge from the dark

---

Final Thought

With light painting, you're not just observing the world—you're actively shaping how it's seen. You've gone from finding light in unlikely places to creating it where none existed.

Now that's power.

Day 29 Reflective Journal Pages

Use these prompts to reflect after each lesson or at the end of each week. There's no right or wrong way to answer—let your thoughts flow honestly and creatively.

Day 29: Finding Light in Unlikely Places

1. What did I observe about the light today?

2. What surprised or challenged me during this lesson?

3. Which image felt the strongest—and why?

4. What would I do differently if I repeated this exercise?

5. Notes, thoughts, or ideas sparked today:

[Space for writing or sketching]

Day 30: Your Light, Your Voice

"Technique gives you tools. Voice gives you purpose."

Why This Matters

After 29 days of learning to observe, shape, and compose with light, you've built more than just technical skills—you've started uncovering something deeper: your photographic voice.

Your voice is that subtle but unmistakable thread that runs through your work. It's not just how you use light, but why. It's the feeling behind your choices, the stories you're drawn to, and the way you see the world. Voice is not something you chase—it's something you uncover through consistent attention, honest curiosity, and personal reflection.

This final lesson brings it all together: your growth, your choices, your light.

What You'll Learn Today

- How to reflect on your creative journey over the last 30 days
- How to identify patterns and preferences in your use of light
- How to begin defining your visual voice through intentional shooting
- How to carry this practice forward into your future photography

Key Concepts: What Is a Photographic Voice?

Your voice is a blend of:

- What you notice (light, emotion, shape, stillness, chaos)

- How you frame it (tight or wide, intimate or abstract)

- Why you shoot (for story, for mood, for memory, for meaning)

- What your light reveals—and what it hides

It shows up not in one image, but in the patterns across your body of work.

📌 Voice is not what you imitate. It's what you return to—again and again—when no one's watching.

Step-by-Step Exercise: Discovering Your Voice Through Light

Today's exercise is part creative review, part reflective shoot. You'll identify how light has shaped your style—and create one final photo that represents where you are right now.

What You Need

- Your camera

- A quiet space or time for reflection

- Your favorite 5–10 images from this 30-day journey

- A journal or notes app

Step 1: Review Your Journey

Look through the images you've created this month. Choose 5–10 that feel especially meaningful to you—not necessarily the most perfect, but the most you.

Ask:

- What kind of light am I drawn to (soft, bold, golden, moody)?

- What emotions show up in my work?

256

- What subjects or scenes do I return to most often?

- What do my images feel like—and what do they say about me?

Write down 3–5 words or phrases that describe your emerging voice (e.g., quiet strength, luminous solitude, tension in stillness, bold geometry, soft wonder).

Step 2: Choose Your Light, Intentionally

Now choose a light scenario that reflects those words. Don't wait for the perfect conditions—create or find light that resonates with the feelings you've just identified.

Your job today isn't to make the most impressive photo—it's to make one that feels like you.

Step 3: Create Your Final Image

Set up your scene—subject, background, light—and give yourself time.

- Compose deliberately

- Embrace the shadows you used to avoid

- Highlight what matters to you

- Include just enough—or leave most of it in mystery

Take a single photo. Or three. Or fifteen. But choose one to represent today.

Step 4: Title and Describe It

Give your final image a title that reflects your intent—not your subject.

Then write a short reflection (1–3 sentences) that completes the phrase:

"This is how I see light, and this is what I want it to say…"

You can keep this private—or share it with others as a statement of creative direction.

Step 5: Celebrate and Continue

You've completed 30 days of deep, mindful photography practice. That alone is worth celebrating.

But this isn't the end. It's the beginning of a practice—a mindset—that can grow with you for years to come. You now have the tools, the awareness, and the creative momentum to keep discovering how light shapes not just your photographs—but your point of view.

Why This Will Make Your Photos Better

This final challenge shifts you from being a student of light to being a creator with intention. It moves you from skill to style. From control to expression.

Because when you understand how you see, everything you create becomes more honest, more personal—and more powerful.

Final Daily Practice

- •Create a photo today using your light, in your way
- •Title it
- •Complete this sentence: "My voice is emerging in light that…"
- •Save it somewhere visible—to remind you how far you've come

Week 4 Reflection: Creative Challenges

In this final week, you pushed past the familiar and stepped fully into your creativity. You experimented with minimal light, color temperature, unusual light sources, abstraction, and visual storytelling. These weren't just exercises in technique—they were invitations to trust your instincts, to explore mood, to make meaning. Through layered light, night scenes, reflections, and repetition, you discovered that photography is not only about what you see—but how you interpret it. You've begun to develop a voice: shaped by curiosity, strengthened by skill, and expressed through light. This is the heart of photographic growth—where your tools meet your vision, and where your images begin to reflect not just the world, but your place in it.

Final Thought

You've reached the end of 30 Days of Light—but in many ways, this is only the beginning. Over these past weeks, you've learned how to observe light, control exposure, compose with intention, and express emotion through your images. More importantly, you've learned how to slow down, to see the world with more attention, and to photograph with purpose. You've spent 30 days exploring the way light moves through the world—and through your lens. But more than that, you've started to understand how it moves through you.

This book wasn't just about improving your technical skills—it was about helping you uncover your photographic voice. The one that's shaped by what catches your eye, what stirs your curiosity, and how light moves through your unique way of seeing.

You now carry the tools to make meaningful photographs in any condition, with any subject. But what matters most is that you keep showing up—with your camera, your attention, and your love for the process. Let light continue to guide you. Let curiosity continue to lead you. And know that every frame you make from here on out carries a piece of your vision, your growth, and your journey. From now on, when you lift your camera, you're not just capturing light. You're shaping it. You're speaking through it. You're honoring your voice.

Welcome to the next chapter of your photographic journey.

Thank you for walking this path with me.

—Carol Fox Henrichs

Day 30 Final Reflective Journal Page

Use these prompts to reflect after each lesson or at the end of each week. There's no right or wrong way to answer—let your thoughts flow honestly and creatively.

Day 30: Your Light, Your Voice

1. What did I observe about the light today?

2. What surprised or challenged me during this lesson?

3. Which image felt the strongest—and why?

4. What would I do differently if I repeated this exercise?

5. Notes, thoughts, or ideas sparked today:

[Space for writing or sketching]

Here are five thoughtfully crafted bonus lessons (Days 31–35) for **30 Days of Light**, each building on prior skills while offering fresh challenges to deepen creativity and personal style.

Day 31: Light Through Layers

"Depth is not just in space—it's in how light filters and shifts."

Objective:

Explore how light interacts with semi-transparent or layered materials to create depth and softness.

Instructions:

- •Choose materials like curtains, lace, plastic, foliage, or glass.
- •Shoot light passing through at least two layers.
- •Experiment with side light, backlight, and shallow depth of field.
- •Try layering objects (e.g. shooting through grass or leaves toward a subject).

Focus: Atmosphere, softness, visual depth.

Day 32: Weather as Light Modifier

"Light doesn't change just by time—it shifts with the sky."

Objective:

Photograph a subject or scene in a specific weather condition and notice how light behaves.

Instructions:

- •Choose one weather scenario: fog, rain, overcast, clear sun, or storm light.
- •Observe how shadows, highlights, and colors shift.
- •Compose to highlight how the quality of light changes emotion.

Focus: Mood, tone, weather-dependent light quality.

Day 33: Light and Color Harmony

"When light reveals color with intention, your image sings."

Objective:

Use color theory to match or contrast your subject with the light's tone (warm/cool).

Instructions:

- Shoot with warm or cool lighting (golden hour, shade, or artificial light).
- Choose a subject with complementary or analogous colors.
- Compose so the color and light work together, not compete.

Focus: Color harmony, emotional tone, storytelling through hue.

Day 34: Recreate a Favorite Photo with Your Own Light

"Imitation isn't copying—it's learning to see with precision."

Objective:

Choose a favorite image (yours or someone else's) and try to recreate its lighting style.

Instructions:

- Analyze the light direction, quality, and intensity of the original.
- Set up a similar lighting situation with your own subject.
- Adjust until your image captures a similar mood—even if the content differs.

Focus: Observation, lighting replication, intentional shooting.

Day 35: Revisit a Previous Lesson with New Light

> "Growth is measured not just in new skills—but in how you see familiar things differently."

Objective:

Return to any lesson from Days 1–30 and shoot it again with a different light source or time of day.

Instructions:

- Choose one favorite lesson (e.g., silhouettes, repetition, single light source).

- Redo the exercise at a new time of day, or with different lighting (natural vs. artificial).

- Compare both results side by side.

Focus: Creative evolution, reflection, visual growth.

30 Days of Light Extras:

Reflective Journaling Prompts

Use the prompts below to deepen your understanding of your growth, challenges, and creative direction from the past 30 days:

1. What surprised me most about working with light was...

2. A photo I made this month that felt truly "mine" was...

3. My favorite kind of light to work with now is...

4. When I struggled most during this journey, I learned...

5. The type of mood I return to most often in my images is...

6. The technical skill I improved the most was...

7. If I could re-do one day's challenge, I'd choose Day ___ because...

8. Three words that describe my current photographic voice are...

9. I now define "good light" as...

10. Moving forward, I want to explore light in these new ways:

Lessons Grouped by Skill, Topic, or Environment

Lessons Requiring or Ideal for Night Photography

Day 11: Low Light Mastery

Day 24: Night Photography Without Flash

Day 29: Finding Light in Unlikely Places

Lessons That Can Optionally Be Practiced at Night

Day 22: Minimal Light, Maximum Mood

Day 26: Visual Storytelling with a Single Light Source

Lessons byBy Technical Skill Focus

Exposure & Camera Control

Day 8: The Exposure Triangle

Day 9: Aperture and Depth of Field

Day 10: Freezing and Blurring Motion

Day 11: Low Light Mastery

Day 12: Histogram Check

Day 13: Exposure Bracketing

Day 14: Metering Modes

Composition and Framing

Day 7: The Direction of Light

Day 15: Silhouettes

Day 16: Shadows as Shape

Day 20: Light and the Rule of Thirds

Day 21: Framing with Light and Shadow

Lessons By Narrative Purpose

Telling Stories with Light

Day 19: Leading the Eye with Light

Day 20: Light and the Rule of Thirds

Day 21: Framing with Light and Shadow

Day 26: Visual Storytelling with a Single Light Source

Day 27: Creating a Visual Series with Light

Day 30: Your Light, Your Voice

Evoking Emotion Through Light

Day 22: Minimal Light, Maximum Mood

Day 23: Color of Light: Warm, Cool & Emotional

Day 25: Abstracting Reality with Light and Shadow

Day 29: Finding Light in Unlikely Places

Lessons By Lighting Conditions

Daylight-Focused

Day 1: Finding the Light

Day 3: Golden Hour Magic

Day 4: Shade and Open Shadow

Day 6: High Noon Contrast

Low Light / Artificial Light

Day 11: Low Light Mastery

Day 17: Window Light Portraits

Day 18: Using Reflected and Bounced Light

Day 24: Night Photography Without Flash

Day 29: Finding Light in Unlikely Places

Lessons By Level of Creative Interpretation Required

Foundational / Observation-Based

Day 1: Finding the Light

Day 2: Hard vs. Soft Light

Day 7: The Direction of Light

Day 12: Histogram Check

Day 14: Metering Modes

Exploratory / Creative Practice

Day 15: Silhouettes

Day 16: Shadows as Shape

Day 22: Minimal Light, Maximum Mood

Day 25: Abstracting Reality with Light and Shadow

Day 30: Your Light, Your Voice

Beginner-Friendly Path Through 30 Days of Light

This curated path highlights 20 lessons from 30 Days of Light that are most accessible, practical, and empowering for photographers who are just starting out. The path introduces key concepts in light, exposure, and composition while building technical skill gradually.

Week 1: Learning to See the Light

Build awareness of how light behaves and how it affects your photos.

Day 1: Finding the Light
Day 2: Hard vs. Soft Light
Day 3: Golden Hour Magic
Day 4: Shade and Open Shadow
Day 5: Backlighting Basics
Day 7: The Direction of Light

Week 2: Camera Basics & Exposure Essentials

Gain control over how your camera sees and captures light.

Day 8: The Exposure Triangle
Day 9: Aperture and Depth of Field
Day 10: Freezing and Blurring Motion
Day 18: Using Reflected and Bounced Light
Day 17: Window Light Portraits

Week 3: Light for Better Composition

Learn to place light—and your subject—for stronger storytelling.

Day 19: Leading the Eye with Light
Day 20: Light and the Rule of Thirds
Day 21: Framing with Light and Shadow
Day 16: Shadows as Shape
Day 15: Silhouettes

Week 4: Creative Confidence & Style

Experiment with style, storytelling, and personal voice using light.

Day 22: Minimal Light, Maximum Mood
Day 23: Color of Light: Warm, Cool & Emotional
Day 27: Creating a Visual Series with Light
Day 30: Your Light, Your Voice

Optional for Continued Growth (Intermediate Skills) Once you're comfortable with manual settings, revisit these:

- •Day 6: High Noon Contrast

- •Day 11: Low Light Mastery

- •Day 12: Histogram Check

- •Day 13: Exposure Bracketing

- •Day 14: Metering Modes

- •Day 24: Night Photography Without Flash

- •Day 25: Abstracting Reality with Light and Shadow

Tip for Beginners: You don't need to complete all lessons in order—take your time, revisit exercises, and allow your curiosity to guide you. Each day is a new chance to grow and see light differently.

Advanced Photographer Path Through 30 Days of Light

This curated path highlights 20 lessons from 30 Days of Light best suited for experienced photographers looking to refine their technical control, creative vision, and storytelling using light. This track emphasizes manual settings, artistic experimentation, and narrative depth.

Week 1: Mastering Light's Behavior

Deepen your ability to analyze, shape, and exploit light conditions.

Day 1: Finding the Light
Day 2: Hard vs. Soft Light
Day 3: Golden Hour Magic
Day 5: Backlighting Basics
Day 6: High Noon Contrast
Day 7: The Direction of Light

Week 2: Precision with Exposure and Control

Enhance your technical mastery and confidence in varied lighting scenarios.

Day 8: The Exposure Triangle
Day 9: Aperture and Depth of Field
Day 10: Freezing and Blurring Motion
Day 11: Low Light Mastery
Day 12: Histogram Check
Day 13: Exposure Bracketing
Day 14: Metering Modes

Week 3: Light as a Storytelling Tool

Use light deliberately to direct attention, create structure, and evoke emotion.

Day 15: Silhouettes
Day 16: Shadows as Shape

Day 19: Leading the Eye with Light
Day 20: Light and the Rule of Thirds
Day 21: Framing with Light and Shadow

Week 4: Creative Exploration & Artistic Voice

Experiment with abstraction, series work, color control, and mood-driven lighting.

Day 22: Minimal Light, Maximum Mood
Day 23: Color of Light: Warm, Cool & Emotional
Day 24: Night Photography Without Flash
Day 25: Abstracting Reality with Light and Shadow
Day 26: Visual Storytelling with a Single Light Source
Day 27: Creating a Visual Series with Light
Day 28: Light and Repetition
Day 29: Finding Light in Unlikely Places
Day 30: Your Light, Your Voice

Optional Revisit for Fine-Tuning Simplicity Even advanced photographers benefit from occasional back-to-basics exercises:

- •Day 4: Shade and Open Shadow

- •Day 17: Window Light Portraits

- •Day 18: Using Reflected and Bounced Light

Tip for Advanced Photographers: Use this path to push the boundaries of your habits. Focus on expressing emotion through lighting choices and developing consistency in how your images feel—not just how they're exposed.

www.ingramcontent.com/pod-product-compliance
Lightning Source LLC
Chambersburg PA
CBHW060450290526
45791CB00001B/48